AN UNFORGETTABLE STORY
OF COURAGE AND LOVE

Something for Joey is based on actual events in the lives of John Cappelletti, the football player, and his kid brother Joey, a victim of leukemia.

As a rising football star at Pennsylvania State, and as a naturally warm and generous person, John became Joey's idol. The kid brother lived for football weekends when he could see his big brother star on the field. But the older brother was in turn inspired by Joey's courage in dealing with pain every moment of his life. In accepting the 1973 Heisman Trophy, awarded annually to the best college player, John Cappelletti startled an audience of dignitaries and celebrities with a tear-filled and moving tribute to Joey, who died in April 1976. This book tells the true, courageous story of the football hero and his heroic young brother.

SOMETHING
for
JOEY

**Story and Teleplay by
JERRY McNEELY**

**Novelization by
RICHARD E. PECK**

Published by
Dell Laurel-Leaf
an imprint of
Random House Children's Books
a division of Random House, Inc.
1540 Broadway
New York, New York 10036

Visit us on the Web! www.randomhouse.com/teens

**Educators and librarians, for a variety of teaching tools,
visit us at www.randomhouse.com/teachers**

ISBN: 0-553-27199-7

Reprinted by arrangement with Bantam Books

Printed in the United States of America

October 2001

OPM 44 43 42 41

joey is diagnosed with lukemia

PROLOGUE

Two brothers. A family. A public ceremony at which years of love and concern culminated in a sharp, shining moment. During the days that followed that ceremony millions shared in the moment through newspaper and television reports. Many told the story to one another and briefly relived the glow of it. But when had the story begun?

Start where you like. Begin with John Cappelletti's arrival in America, four years old at the time, clutching the hands of his immigrant parents. Or on a Saturday afternoon nineteen years later, when the grown John Cappelletti married Anne Bianco in Philadelphia's St. Mary Magdalene Church, at the same altar where Anne's mother had been married thirty-five years before.

With the arrival of Martin, John and Anne's first-born, the young couple became a family. John Jr. followed, then Michael, and Jean, and Joey. And though the word "family" doesn't change over the years, the meaning of it, and the sense of what that family is, grew and deepened with each new child.

During those years the children learned from their parents, and from one another, and became individuals: Martin, bright and studious, more mercurial than the others; John and Michael, each in his own way a fine athlete; Jean, the dark-eyed replica of her mother; and Joey. No one can guess what they might have become without the experiences they shared. What they are—what they have together—is the story.

On December 13th, 1973, John Cappelletti, Jr., stood before nearly four thousand well-wishers in the Grand Ballroom of the New York Hilton Hotel and shocked that sophisticated crowd into stunned, tear-filled silence, by presenting his younger brother Joey with a gift. He dedicated to Joey a trophy he had just won.

The trophy itself wasn't the gift, only the symbol of a richer gift that can't be photographed, or weighed, or physically handled.

This is a true story, about a remarkable family. A story about two brothers, John and Joey: the first a superbly-conditioned athlete of twenty-one; the other, half that age and suffering from leukemia.

This is a love story.

FALL 1971

1

A college football weekend is special. At Pennsylvania State University, it usually begins early on Friday afternoon. Local fans stroll to the practice fields located beside the large dormitory complex called East Halls. Alumni, parents and friends of the team begin arriving, parking their cars in one of the large, open grass fields nearby. Carrying cameras on bright days, on rainy days huddled under brightly colored golf umbrellas or hunched over in yellow slickers, they gather to watch the Friday afternoon drills. For many, it's their only chance to see the team close up, to get a pre-game look at who's healthy and ready for Saturday's action. It's a chance to start building the heady, exhilarating tension that reaches its climax on Saturday afternoon. This September Friday was no different. Many attentive fans nodded to one another. The regulars were there.

Seated in temporary bleachers near the practice field, wearing light jackets, sweaters, shirtsleeves, thirty or thirty-five people watched together in the cool autumn air. Nearer the field, leaning against the rust-red pickets of a snowfence that separated the actual playing surface from the spectators, stood two local football fans in their forties. One wore a gray windbreaker, the other a checked jacket and an orange hunting cap perched askew on top of his bald head. Watching the drill, they paid no attention to the dark-haired boy of eight who stood nearby.

On the field, the Nittany Lions clapped and shouted encouragement to one another as they ran through the light, day-before-the-game workout. They wore sweatpants, numbered jerseys and helmets but no pads. It was a no-contact drill, a two-thirds speed imitation of a real game, a rehearsal of various offensive and de-

3

fensive formations. At one end of the field, two punt-
ers alternated sending spirals lofting high against the
blue September sky, while pairs of offensive ends and
special-team linesmen sprinted downfield under those
punts to tag the back who caught the ball.

Meanwhile, nearer the two local fans, the Penn
State offensive backfield ran through plays, brushing
up already well-drilled and nearly automatic moves.
But there was no real contact. Linesmen pulled their
blocks and lunged up off their three-point stances into
a high crouch, their folded arms extended in front of
them to ward off the defensive linesmen charging at
them.

Offensive and defensive coaches, all specialists,
worked with different units. At the west end of the
field a place-kicker practiced field goals from some
twenty yards out. One after another, balls popped
from the holder's grip to tumble end-over-end between the white-painted uprights.

To someone unfamiliar with football—to a Euro-
pean, say, used to watching the clean, open sweep of a
soccer line—the scene might have appeared chaotic.
Too much activity, perhaps, in too many places, of
too many kinds. But circling through the workout
was the head coach, Joe Paterno. A slight, dark-haired
man in glasses, he was obviously in charge. Though
the players shouted, he spoke quietly—in a voice that
carried the authority earned in twenty-two years as a
fixture at Penn State. Joe Paterno was one of America's
most successful college coaches.

With a dozen different drills simultaneously underway on different parts of the field, it didn't seem possible that one man could keep his eye on them all, but
Joe Paterno did. From time to time he shouted. "Stay
with your block, Pete! You came off too soon!" Or he
walked over to one of the halfbacks, bent his knees
slightly to lean forward and pantomime a position
he wanted the back to try. Instructions over, he passed
on to the next group.

The two fans at the fence were watching the coach,
each trying to impress the other with his inside knowl-

edge of what was going on. The man in the orange cap said, "I had a nice chat with Coach Paterno the other day."

"Sure you did."

The short boy now kneeling beside them, and peering between pickets in the snowfence, looked up.

"Well, I did."

"And you told him what's what, didn't you?"

"No," said Orange-cap. "I only meant, I ran into him in the drugstore. We stood there and talked a long time."

"What about?"

The boy glanced from one man to the other.

"Huh?"

"I said, what did you talk about?" The man turned from the field and fixed his friend with a stare. "Come on, let me have the whole story."

"Oh, you know—how the team was doing, like that. We just talked about . . . well, you know."

Paterno, watching the drill, moved closer to the sidelines. The second man looked at his boasting friend expectantly and with a small gesture pointed out that the coach was standing within earshot. Still the boy watched with interested eyes. Finally the braggart, challenged by his friend's stare, gathered his determination and said, "How's it going, Coach?"

Puzzled, Paterno looked around for a moment before locating the source of the greeting. "We're working on it," he said. Then Paterno noticed the boy. He grinned. He turned away from the players and walked over to the fence. "Joey," he said. "How you doing, buddy?"

"Hi, Coach."

Paterno reached over the fence to shake Joey's hand. "See you in the locker room tomorrow?"

"You bet!"

The two men stared at Joey and the coach.

"Thataboy," Paterno said. Then he turned back to the drilling players.

"You're a friend of his?" Orange-cap said to the boy, pointing at Paterno.

"Yes, sir."

"He lets you in the locker room and everything, huh?"

"Yes, he does."

The other man said, "Well. The kid's a regular celebrity."

"Not me," Joey told him. "But my brother is. He's on the team."

"Yeah?" said the boaster. "What's his name?"

"John Cappelletti. He plays defensive back."

The man thought a moment, then said, "I don't think I've heard of him."

Joey's answer was quiet but confident. "You will. There he is now."

A pass play was developing in front of them. One of the defensive backs back-pedaled toward the sidelines, his eyes on the flanker who'd faked inside and was now sprinting a deep-out pattern. The ball was in the air; the back cut left to tighten his coverage on the flanker but his feet crossed with the move and he slammed to the turf a few feet away from his embarrassed little brother. Muttering, he lay on his back while the grinning flanker cradled the ball in his huge hands and slowed to a trot in the clear.

Joey glanced up uneasily at the two men, then spoke quietly. "Nice try, Yo-yo."

John Cappelletti lay on the ground a second longer, a wry grin on his face as he looked at Joey. "I'll get it together one of these days, Hoss." Then he sprang to his feet and trotted back to the defensive huddle.

Slight, slender, Joey Cappelletti no longer looked like the sort of boy you nickname "Hoss," though he had as a very young child, when his stocky build had earned him the nickname taken from TV's *Bonanza,* and "Hoss" Cartwright. He watched his brother until he couldn't pretend not to hear any more: his mother was calling him from the stands and he knew he'd better respond. But first he waved to her, hoping that would be enough.

"Don't you bother Johnny," she called. "Come back here."

Joey looked up once more at the two men and their approving smiles, then ran to the bleachers.

The rest of his family was watching from there. His father, John Cappelletti, Sr.—a tall, slender man in his forties—had a warm smile on his face as Joey approached. Beside John Sr. sat Anne Cappelletti, a pretty, dark-haired woman a bit younger than her husband. Joey's sister Jean, a sophomore in high school, and Michael—a broad-shouldered high school athlete—were next. And at the end of the wooden bench sat Marty, the oldest of the Cappelletti children, out of college for a year and a reporter on a local newspaper. Beside Marty, holding his hand, was his wife Joyce. Striking enough in any setting, Joyce really stood out now—a blue-eyed blonde among the dark-haired Cappellettis.

Joyce and Marty slid to one side and Joyce patted the bench, inviting Joey to join them.

He pointed toward the field. "Mom, I can see better over there. Can't I go back?"

His father nodded.

"Don't get in the way," Anne said.

But Joey had already bolted off, his eyes on his brother, who was drifting back to cover a pass receiver angling downfield into his zone. Both John and the receiver leaped at the same instant, a flurry of scrambling arms in mid-air. When they hit the turf it was John who clutched the ball to his chest.

Clapping and cheering wildly, Joey couldn't resist a gloating glance at the two men beside him, both still standing there. They looked from Joey to Number 22, proudly holding the ball aloft in one hand as he trotted back to the line of scrimmage. Joey stopped short of saying "I told you so," but the expression was there in his eyes.

Paterno blew a pair of shrill blasts on his whistle. "All right, that's it," he shouted. "Two laps and inside!" Then he began the long walk to the fieldhouse across the way. His assistants joined him in low-voiced conversation as they crossed the field, while the players began to circle the track. Some sprinted as if eager to complete their two laps and head for a hot shower; others trotted, talking as they finished out the laps, reluctant to leave the field. But Joey's eyes were fixed on one figure—the number 22 in white numerals on the back of his navy blue jersey—his brother John, running with the others.

The rest of the Cappelletti family stepped down from the bleachers and began to walk along the fence toward the boy. As John neared them in his circuit of the field he reached over the low fence and seized Joey under the arms. Almost effortlessly he hoisted his brother up and onto the field.

It was one of Joey's good days. Joey spent most of the week looking forward to Saturday, when he could watch John play football. And on days like this, on those rare occasions when the entire family came up to Penn State to watch Friday practice as well as the Saturday game, Joey's personal sky was brightest of all. *His* week had a three-day weekend.

John took his hand, and they crossed the nearly empty practice field toward the locker room. Even without pads, John was fully twice Joey's size. No one could misunderstand the implication of strength present in his broad shoulders. But when he shortened his stride to match Joey's and draped an arm around the younger boy, an observer would have noticed the tenderness there as well. They crossed the field, John's head canted and a soft smile on his lips as he listened to Joey's excited chatter.

2

Upper Darby is a suburb of Philadelphia, a community of two- and three-story homes of stone, stucco and frame construction. The Cappelletti house stands behind a low privet hedge that separates the lawn from the sidewalk. A pair of bay windows filled with potted house plants swells from the front of the house, one on either side of the central door. On this late November afternoon, the street unseasonably warm even under the shade of the large elms that bordered it, the front door stood ajar. A young boy's laughter drifted out into the street.

"You may be a big-deal football player, but as a wrestler, you're the pits!" It was Joey speaking, between bouts of laughter.

Joey and his older brother John were wrestling on the living room floor. John lay pinned to the mat—a floral-patterned carpet. Joey straddled him victoriously, his knees resting on John's spread-eagled arms.

"Let me tell you something, pal," John said. "You're all wind and no muscle." He grunted heavily, seized Joey's shoulders and flipped the boy over onto the floor with a loud thud.

"What are you two up to in there?" Anne Cappelletti called from the kitchen, on her way to find out.

"Try that again and see how far you get," Joey said.

"Johnny, now stop it!" Anne entered, still dusting her hands on her apron.

Joey said, "I'm all right, Mom."

"Just getting a lesson in humility," John said, grinning.

"It's almost time to leave for the hospital. Go change your clothes, Joey."

"Okay." Joey clambered to his feet. Walking past John, laid back on the floor again, Joey nudged him with his toe. "I'll get you next time."

"Boy, are you lucky she came in," John said. "Talk about next time! Next time I'll splatter you against the wall."

Joey only laughed and trotted up the stairs.

Their mother shook her head, then returned to the kitchen.

John lay on the floor watching her go. Frowning, he pondered for a moment. Then he followed her.

The kitchen was light and airy, its warmth a reflection of Anne's own. Paneled cabinets, installed by John Sr., hung above the counter tops. The window over the sink looked into the back yard, where a small, above-ground swimming pool was visible, drained now for the winter and covered with a plastic sheet. Anne was putting the finishing touches to a casserole. She crumbled bread crumbs in her hand to top it.

John hesitated in the doorway. Then, casually, he walked over and picked a sliver of onion from the casserole to chew on. He swung around to lean against the counter. "You all right, Mom?"

"What kind of question is that?" Turning away from John, she fussed with the casserole.

"You seem kind of edgy, that's all. I mean, you're the one who's always wandering around this kitchen like you own the place, singing and—"

"Not today." She still wouldn't meet his concerned eyes.

"I'm sorry. Just a question."

"I guess I didn't hear it." Anne smiled wryly. "What did you ask me?"

"Why are you so down today?" He pulled out a chair and sat at the table to face her, chin propped in cupped hands.

"Because I work under such tension."

"You?" John laughed.

Anne took the Pyrex dish and slid it into the oven. "Sure. If I don't get this in the oven in time, supper's late and I get yelled at."

John smiled but he wasn't ready to be so easily put off. There was an edginess about her he couldn't define. "Joey's okay, isn't he?"

Anne twisted the dish around on the oven rack, keeping her face averted. "He's fine, as far as I can tell."

The front door slammed. "Anybody home?" John Sr. called out.

Rolling her eyes for John's benefit, Anne answered the familiar voice. "No. We all left for Bermuda!"

"Why didn't you take me along?" John Senior—Dad Cappelletti—entered the kitchen with his jacket in one hand, a lunch bucket in the other. He was dressed in gray workclothes and steel-toed safety shoes. A folding rule protruded from his shirt pocket in a nest of pencils and ballpoint pens. He took a look at his son and said, "I thought you were going back to school today."

"No, I had a paper to write. I thought it would be quieter here than at the FIJI house."

Dad nodded, draping his jacket over a kitchen chair.

"*John!*" Anne said.

"What?"

"How can I ask the children to hang up their clothes when you do something like that?"

"What did I do?"

"That's a chair, not a hanger."

Dad smiled. "Don't you think my bad habits have already corrupted the children beyond redemption?" He patted Anne affectionately on the shoulder. She acknowledged the pats, but she didn't return the smile. Her somberness puzzled him.

"Dinner's in the oven," said John. "Casserole."

"When are you going back to school?" Dad asked.

"I'll get up early in the morning."

"Make sure it's early enough you don't miss any classes," Anne said.

John exchanged shrugs with his father. Nothing they could do seemed to divert Anne from whatever problem occupied her mind. Her present attitude was so unlike her usual cheerfulness that both men were puzzled. Since nothing they could say would make her explain, they turned to her and waited.

Anne gave a little sigh. "I'm sorry," she said. "Joey said something a while ago that . . . well, it upset me."

"What did he say?" Dad asked.

"If you must know, he asked me to promise he wouldn't have to go to the hospital next year."

The two men nodded their understanding. Both of them would have done anything in their power to help Joey; neither of them would lie to him. The promise Joey asked for was the one promise that no one could make.

Even adults carry the sense of personal immortality.

How could an eight-year-old be expected to understand the full import of a disease whose name he couldn't even spell? He knew he was ill, but most of the time, because he felt well, that knowledge was then pushed to the back of his mind. Of course he wanted reassurance. And it was Anne who had to answer Joey's bewildered questions. The two men weren't with him all day, as his mother was. Dad was home every night after work, of course, and weekends. But for John a trip home from Penn State was a rare treat. Most of his time was spent either in football practice or in class. His visits home in fact were holidays for Joey, a chance for the two of them to play together, to enjoy each other's company. But it was Anne who cared for Joey, whether John was home or at school. No brief, weekend excitement could erase the painful knowledge she carried with her all the time.

"Days like this," she said, "I wonder if we did the right thing."

With quiet authority her husband said, "We did, and you know it, Anne."

"What are you two talking about?" John asked.

"Oh, nothing."

"Come on, Dad," John persisted. "What is it?"

His father deliberated for a moment. It was characteristic of him never to waste words, but when he did speak to speak with clear and quiet authority. "When the doctors first told us Joey had leukemia," he said, "they gave us two choices. We could try to keep him as comfortable as possible and let the whole thing take its course. Or we—"

"Six months . . . maybe," Anne said.

Dad nodded. "That's right. If we did nothing, six months. Or we could put him in the experimental program at Children's Hospital. They couldn't promise anything, except that there'd be some pain."

"But they never said how *much!*" Anne turned away. She felt so useless! Her husky voice had already revealed the pessimism she tried to conceal.

"Anne, they didn't know how much," Dad said. He laid a protective hand on her shoulder.

"You mean, you had to decide that?" John asked. "Without knowing what it all meant?"

"There was no decision," Dad said. "We told them to do whatever they could. We figured, as long as Joey was alive we'd have hope." He looked at Anne for confirmation. She nodded reluctantly. "We still feel that way."

There was nothing to say to that. At that moment, John understood better than he ever had before the burden his parents carried. He understood that the past five years of Joey's life had been granted the boy because of the decision his parents had made—five extra years, but at the cost of painful, and only delaying, procedures.

"Hey, Mom," he said. "Let me take Joey to the hospital today."

"No, I'm fine." She straightened her shoulders and smiled with fresh resolution.

"I know you are. But I'll still take him. With all the free time that'll give you, you can make me a carrot cake."

"It's already made," she said, a touch of lively good humor back in her voice.

"Good. Then you can paint the garage." John went to the foot of the stairs in the front of the house and called: "Move your boots, Hoss! You've got a new driver today!"

"Be there in a minute!" Joey shouted.

John turned around, on his way back to the kitchen. But he stopped short. His parents were framed in the doorway. His father, erect and tall, looked reflectively into the distance as Anne leaned against him, her head on his shoulder. There was no anguish in her pose—only resignation, the calm acceptance that is its own kind of peace.

They drove on WestChester Pike toward Children's Hospital for Joey's weekly visit. Joey, on the front seat beside John, was all squirming energy. He bounced on the seat, pointing at the sights as they passed—a super foreign car, a new garage under construction, a telephone lineman high up a pole leaning back against his safety belt. He was enjoying both the ride itself and the chance to have a "man-to-man" talk with John. His steady chatter made it difficult for John to remember how ill Joey really was.

"I still think it's dumb," Joey said. "You were all-State quarterback in high school. Why did they make you a defensive back."

"Ahhh, the coach knows what he's doing."

"Is it better than playing linebacker?"

"Well, there's less head-bumping, for one thing. Yeah, I guess it's better."

"But not better than running back."

"You never let up for a second, do you?" John grinned. "No, I guess it's not. I'd like a chance to carry the ball once in a while."

"Okay," Joey said. "Just tell the coach." He couldn't imagine anyone refusing his brother anything.

"It doesn't work that way, Hoss. There are a couple of studs out there in front of me, remember? Am I going to beat out Lydell Mitchell? Franco Harris? There's no way Paterno is going to put me ahead of those two guys."

Joey struggled to suppress a mischievous grin. "You're not good enough, admit it."

John picked up the needling. "Uh-huh. Let's wait till you go out for football. Then you can yap."

As quick as a heartbeat, Joey turned solemn. "Okay," he said.

John glanced at the boy, disturbed by the tone in his voice and concerned that he had hurt Joey's feelings. When they began to rag each other, no matter how light their conversations were, John held in the back of his mind the recognition that Joey might never play football, might never even go to high school. And at times like that, there were often unintended meanings in his most light-hearted remarks.

"Got any more of that bubblegum?" John said. Anything to change the subject.

Joey fumbled in his shirt pocket and withdrew a piece of bubblegum. Staring out of the window, he offered it to John.

"Hey, peel it for me, will you? I ought to keep one hand on the wheel, or we'll wind up plowing somebody's front yard."

Joey stripped the paper off and handed the gum to John.

They drove in silence for several blocks.

Finally, John said, "Do you like this hospital?"

"It's pretty nice. Everybody wears regular clothes, did you know that? Even nurses don't wear uniforms."

"Is that right?" John nudged him.

Joey grinned at the joke he hadn't meant to tell. "Did Mom tell you they put me back a grade in school? A whole year!"

"Yeah, she did."

"They said maybe I can catch up, as long as I don't have to spend too much time in the hospital."

"Well then, let's work on that, what do you say?"

"Yeah." Joey looked out the window, suddenly very thoughtful.

John searched his imagination for a neutral topic of conversation, unhappy again with Joey's mood.

"Otherwise," Joey continued, "I won't be able to go out for football till I'm seventeen!"

John almost burst into relieved laughter. If that was Joey's biggest concern . . . "Right," he said.

"But listen!" Joey was excited. He twisted around in his seat to face his brother. "That could work out okay. By that time, I'll probably be bigger than the other guys!"

"You'll stomp over 'em like King Kong!"

"I'll flatten them. And by then this lousy bone marrow'll be fixed, too."

John reached over to ruffle Joey's hair. The moments of gloom that came over the boy often passed as quickly as they appeared. There was a lot of strength

in Joey, a resilience and spirit that John admired.
Fortunately, at his age, Joey dwelt more on the happy
possibilities of the future, on a boy's concerns: football, the approval of his family, of his brother.

Mere approval wasn't all that was visible in John's
frequent sidelong glances at Joey. There was genuine
admiration, that and pride in his brother's grit and
optimism.

3

The Penn State campus is nearly two hundred miles
from Upper Darby, but the drive to the university
never seemed too long for the Cappellettis. Anticipation shortened the ride. Whether they made the trip
early on Friday—on those rare occasions when everyone in the family had the afternoon free—or on Friday night wasn't finally important. Because it was
Saturday that counted. These shared family experiences were so festive that they worked like a tonic on
Joey. However sick or depressed he might have been
the week before, on Saturday he was irrepressible energy.

His parents in the front seat of the car, Michael
and Jean beside him in the back, Joey noted each
familiar landmark with a broader smile, measuring the
miles. His mood lightened visibly, he talked more and
more as they skirted Harrisburg and began to follow
the wide winding bends of the Susquehanna River up-
stream into the low Tuscarora mountain range east of
Penn State. Joey couldn't wait to get there. Tomorrow, he'd see his brother in action!

The town of State College claimed a resident popu-
lation of 35,000. University enrollment nearly matched
that figure, and Saturday afternoons found more than
58,000 fans packed into Beaver Stadium on the east-

ern edge of the campus. Traffic had begun to fill the small town as early as 8:00 or 9:00 in the morning, coming from western Ohio, West Virginia, Maryland and New York City.

A caravan of loaded cars had turned off Bald Mountain Ridge to wind down State Highway 322 from the west and into the huge bowl of flatland ringed by gently worn mountains: Mt. Nittany northeast, Stone Mountain and Warriors' Ridge to the south.

By noon on the streets bordering the campus, students carrying navy and white paper pompoms had clustered on corners to wait for their friends, then trek east along College Avenue past the T-intersection with Allen Street where a mall, lined with ash and elm trees, stretched left up the hill toward Old Main and the center of campus.

The complex of seven-story dorms called East Hall was wearing full colors: vivid blankets and sheets hung from the windows on all floors; the sheets with dayglow letters sprayed on them, threatening destruction to Syracuse. Beyond the dorms was a large open field crammed with parked cars—the station wagons with their tailgates down as picnic tables . . . or bartops.

It was 12:30, an hour before kickoff, when Joey led the Cappellettis through the maze of parked cars, past knots of roistering picnickers toward the stadium. "C'mon," he shouted. "We'll be late!"

"Joey, you stay with us," Anne called after him. Then she laughed helplessly as Joey dashed on ahead. "Sometimes I think I'm talking to myself," she said.

"He won't get far without these." Michael waved the tickets he carried.

Marty and Joyce had driven up in their own car that morning to meet the rest of the family. A hurried picnic lunch in the parking area—a lunch made more hurried by Joey's eagerness to get into the stadium— had taken only minutes. Salami and cheese and bread and peanut butter, iced tea and coffee, a flurry of paper napkins, paper cups, then everything emptied and packed away. Now, with the crowd growing and excitement in the air rising to an audible hum, they hurried through the east gate into the gray blue bowl.

A crouching blue lion atop a sign proclaiming the season's schedule ushered them in. Underneath the sign, it was a madhouse: Lion boosters passed out lapel buttons; candy butchers and hot dog salesmen barked their wares; souvenir hawkers shouted, "Hey, pennants! I got your pennant here!" "Programs! Yearbooks! Buy your girl a lion!"

The Penn State Blue Band was already assembling behind the bleachers along the south end of the field. Some wore their jackets unbuttoned; others tugged chinstraps tight and noodled on their horns, adding to the din of excited voices. A bass drummer settled the harness straps across his shoulders and tried to get comfortable.

Joey was a whirlwind around his parents. "Can I go tell John we're here?"

His father rested a hand on Joey's shoulder, only in part to get his attention; he wanted to keep track of the scampering boy as well. "You talked to him an hour ago."

"But I want to go into the locker room."

"Later. What if the team comes out and we're not in our seats? What'll John think then?"

"Oh, yeah!" Joey broke free and dashed on ahead.

Michael grinned. "Always know the right thing to say, don't you, Dad?"

"It's called 'psychology,'" Marty said. "Or something."

"Uh-huh. Or something." Dad pointed the way and craned his neck to keep Joey in sight.

The teams poured from a tunnel under the west stands onto the field, Syracuse leading the way in their white visiting uniforms. Applause and scattered cheers greeted them.

And then the Nittany Lions broke onto the field. It wasn't necessary to see them to know they were there. Beaver Stadium exploded in a deep-throated roar that rose in the hazy sunshine and swelled from the stadi-

um to be heard beyond the soccer field, the ice arena
and dorms, all the way to Allen Street. And as the
Blue Band struck up the Penn State fight song, an
ocean of blue and white pompoms waved through the
student cheering sections.

"There he is, Dad! I see him!" Joey shouted.

"I know."

"Joyce? You see? Number Twenty-Two." Joey waved
a hand to guide his sister-in-law's searching gaze.

"Calm down, Hoss," Martin told him. "You'll
wear yourself out before the game starts."

But Joey had already turned away to tug at Jean's
coatsleeve. "D'you think he can see us?"

"I think in a minute I'm going to sit on you!"
Michael said, and lifted the sprawling boy off his
lap to set him upright again.

"Joey?" Anne Cappelletti shook her head. "Peace.
All right?"

"Awww, Mom." Joey subsided from frenzy into
mere excitement, bouncing in his seat with every new
formation the teams made on the field as they went
through their warm-up drills. He kept his seat—
somchow—until the kickoff gave everyone the excuse
to rise shouting. And from that point on, Joey was a
model of fascinated attention.

Penn State scored early in the first quarter, as quarterback John Hufnagel sneaked the ball in from the
three. In the second quarter another 17 points appeared under HOME on the giant scoreboard. After
every point cheerleader Bob Walsh, wearing his lion
costume, dropped flat on the ground and pumped out
a pushup for each point: seven pushups in the first
quarter; then, in the second quarter, ten, after a field
goal raised the score, then seventeen, then twenty-four.
Roaring voices kept count for him, and after the third
Penn State touchdown he was hoisted into the air and
passed from hand to hand all the way up to the top of
the student cheering section.

Watching every play intently, Joey kept a private set
of statistics for the day. At defensive back, Number 22
returned five punts for nearly forty yards and twice

batted down passes that might have gone for touchdowns. Final score for the day: Penn State 31, Syracuse 0; and—in Joey's personal scorebook—John Cappelletti, 1000.

With the long ride home awaiting them, the Cappellettis stopped briefly in the exuberant locker room to say their good-byes to John and exchange a few words with Coach Paterno. Then it was back to the parking lot—nearly empty already—and their cars.

"You can ride back with us if you want to," Martin told Joey.

"Never mind," Anne said. "You two might as well go straight home. This one's got to rest."

"Okay. See you," Marty said.

Joyce kissed Anne and they said good-bye.

After the excitement of the game, the noise and color and jostling crowds, the ride back home was a letdown. Between his brother and sister in the back seat of the car, Joey squirmed. He moved constantly, the way a kitten will circle and twist and circle again, trying to find the most comfortable position. He shifted from hip to hip, and on one of his twisting turns he accidentally kicked Jean's leg.

"Attaboy, Joey," she said. "I think you broke it that time."

The comment was light—more a joke than a complaint—but Joey turned on Jean, near tears. "I can't help it! I was just trying to find a place so my head doesn't hurt!"

"Hey, hey, I'm sorry," Jean said quickly, comforting him. "It's okay."

"C'mon, Hoss, put your head on my lap," Michael said. He twisted sideways and straightened his legs, making more room for Joey.

"Never mind." Joey jerked away. "I'll just sit here and let it hurt!"

"Things getting out of hand back there?" his father asked.

Anne looked at Joey over her shoulder. "Want to come up front?"

"What good would that do?"

"You might be more comfortable."

"No." Joey was sitting very still. "I wish I'd gone back with Marty and Joyce."

Jean, moving farther to her left to make room for him, reached over and eased him down so that his head lay on her lap. "Come on, Joey. Stretch out."

"No problem," Michael said. He pulled Joey's legs up till the boy lay stretched across the seat.

Joey wasn't altogether happy with the arrangement but he let them try to make him comfortable, suddenly feeling so bad that he lacked even the slight strength needed to complain. His hand rubbed listlessly across his closed eyes to brush away a furtive tear he didn't want seen.

Michael and Jean exchanged smiles and shifted once more, seeking out positions they could hold for the long ride ahead. Jean lifted Joey's head to brush the hair off his forehead. Her smile faded.

"Mom," she said quietly. She was looking at Joey. "*Mom?*"

Anne turned her head in response.

"His temperature's up."

"He had a busy day," Anne said. In her voice there was a plea for reassurance—an implied request that Jean confirm the comforting excuse she had seized upon.

"*Really* up, Mom. He's pretty hot."

"John? How much longer?" Anne watched her husband to gauge his reaction to Jean's hushed comment.

"Another two hours. Maybe more."

"Maybe by then—"

"We'll take him to the hospital in the morning," he said. "The next gas station that's open, I'll stop and soak a towel in cool water." He looked at his daughter in the rear-view mirror. "Jean?"

She nodded and cradled Joey's head in her hands.

4

Joey spent a restless night. In the morning his temperature was still up, and though he didn't seem to be in particular pain he was quiet, withdrawn and listless. After his father had gone off to work and the older children to school, Anne bundled Joey into the family car and drove into the city.

Joey was no stranger to hospitals. Along with other children in a special, experimental leukemia program, he had been going to them for five years. Joey suffered these visits with a peculiar kind of stoicism. It was as if he assumed that all children his age went through the same special examinations and suffered the same irritation and pain he endured.

When someone is born blind or loses his sight very early in life, he may grow to adulthood without any real understanding of what sighted people see. The darkness he lives in is a constant condition and, so far as he knows, "normal." And to a large extent, this was the case with Joey. So accustomed to spending his time with doctors who probed and questioned and tried to help him—to no good effect that Joey could recognize—he no longer reacted the way a stranger to pain would react. Hospitals were a normal though unpleasant fact of his life.

There were, too, his friends—many of them in the research program with him, sharing his experiences. To see those few same faces at the hospital cheered Joey up, and helped him forget his own problems. One of his friends, a freckled redhead named Mark, was sitting in a chair in the waiting room when Joey and his mother arrived.

"Hey Joey! Look at this." Mark displayed a new comic book that lay on his lap.

Joey said nothing but walked slowly over and sat down in the chair beside Mark.

"Look what these crazy guys are doing."

Joey glanced at the comic book without interest for a moment and then looked up at his mother. Anne smiled and nodded, encouraging him to talk with Mark.

"See where he drives the car into the wall?" Mark pointed to one of the cartoon panels and giggled happily.

Joey forced a strained smile but winced even at that slight effort.

"You rest, Joey," Anne said, then turned and walked quickly down the tiled corridor to the receptionist's desk, her heels clicking a rapid tattoo.

"Doctor Wingreen's expecting us," she said.

The duty nurse looked up from the clipboard where she was initialing medication dosage records. "Hello, Mrs. Cappelletti." She reached over to push an intercom button.

"Thank you." Smiling, Anne pointed back down the corridor. "I'll be waiting down here with the boys."

"I'll tell the doctor," the nurse called after her.

The waiting area was more a cul-de-sac than a room, a small alcove off the corridor midway between the elevators at one end of the hall and the nurses' station. Anne sat across from the boys and watched Mark trying to entertain Joey. Occasionally she spoke to the two of them, but most of her attention was focussed on Joey, sitting slumped in his chair, one toe idly tracing circles on the white tile floor.

They'd been waiting only ten minutes when the duty nurse entered and said, "Boys, are you ready?"

Mark bounced to his feet. "Which room this time?"

The nurse smiled at his quickness and pointed at a door directly across the hall. To Joey she said, "If you'll come this way, Doctor Wingreen's waiting for you."

Anne watched the two boys, each going to his own examination room. The contrast between them disturbed her. Mark seemed eager to get done with that unpleasant weekly chore, his regular checkup, neither in pain nor depressed—almost happy. Joey, on the other hand, walked with shoulders slumped as he leaned against the nurse's supporting arm. It was all Anne could do to stay in her seat and not run after him, but she knew from past experience how much Joey disliked being coddled. Doctor Wingreen would speak with her as soon as the examination was over. She sat and waited.

Joey entered the doctor's office.

"Feeling a little down today?" Doctor Wingreen asked. A fatherly, balding man in his fifties, he had a weight problem he tried to hide by wearing loose shirts and jackets, a deep love of children that he didn't try to hide at all. He spoke in a soft, calm voice and showed that knack—so rare among adults—of treating his young patients as equals, not patronizing them as little children.

Joey said nothing, but nodded, hiking himself up backward to sit on the examination table with his feet dangling.

"All right, Joey. I'll see what I can discover. If you think of anything I ought to know, tell me, will you?" The doctor nodded to the intern assisting him and took the small penlight offered him. He peered into Joey's eyes, beginning a neurological check at the point where the nervous stystem is most accessible to outside examination.

"You know what this is called?" the intern said. He held up the inflatable canvas armband used to measure blood pressure. "Sphygmomanometer. How's that for a nine-dollar word?" He smiled at Joey, trying to entertain the boy as he worked, but Doctor Wingreen caught the intern's eye and shook his head. Joey was more experienced at examinations than the intern was, and no amount of "charm" would divert him from what was really taking place.

The examination proceeded quickly. To the casual observer it didn't differ markedly from an annual check-up: blood pressure and a blood sample were

taken, the sample sent to the lab for analysis; vision
and hearing were checked; height and weight were
measured and recorded in the thick file bearing Joey's
name.

But in the detailed lab work underway elsewhere in
the hospital there *was* a difference in the examination,
because the technicians there knew exactly what they
were looking for: wild cells, leucocytes in excess. Joey's
blood was checked specifically for hemoglobin and
platelet count—oxygen-carrying red cells and coagulat-
ing elements that prevented his bleeding excessively.

A bone marrow sample was also taken, to determine
whether normal white cells were being produced. The
sample could be drawn from the sternum or breast-
bone, or from a hipbone—by far the most commonly
chosen locale, but in Joey's case, it was taken from
the lower spine or coccyx.

All those tests were a normal part of his periodic
check. Less frequently but still often enough for Anne
to flinch at even thinking of it, a spinal tap was necessary to relieve pressure in Joey's spinal column—and
the accompanying severe headaches. The small amount
of fluid removed was replaced with a smaller amount
of the medication Joey's condition currently called for.

Throughout these tests, even during the painful
spinal tap, Joey remained stoic, as if he was concentrating on some distant time and place where no one had
to probe and lance and knead his aching body. His
body had to be present; but his imagination didn't.
With all the will at his command, Joey tried to focus
on the best of all possible futures.

No matter how Joey responded to the tests and
treatment, they were always painful for Anne. Waiting impatiently to hear the test results, she couldn't
avoid picturing in her mind what Joey might be under-
going behind those closed doors. Her wait was made
worse by the feeling of helplessness it bred in her.

By mid-afternoon, tests were still underway. Then
Doctor Wingreen put Joey in a quiet room to rest for a
while as test results and lab reports were processed. It
was dinnertime before the doctor was able to talk with

Anne. His news was not good. After their brief conversation, she walked out of the hospital to the car—
alone.

At home, Jean and Joyce had cooked dinner. The
family had eaten and were sitting there talking, tense
and anxious for whatever news Anne might bring them.
It was not a typical dinner. Anne's laughter and presence were missing, and so was Joey.

Finally, they heard the front door open.

"Anne? Is that you?" Dad rose to meet her. "How
is he?" Her downcast look was not reassuring—nor was
the absence of Joey.

She pantomimed for patience and led him back to
the others.

Joyce was frozen in the kitchen doorway, holding a
stack of plates. Jean was bent over the table, Michael
still beside her. Marty had just risen. Like figures in a
candid snapshot they waited to hear the news.

Marty was the first to speak. "Where's Joey?"

"They're keeping him in the hospital," Anne said.
"He has the chicken pox."

There was stunned silence. Then Michael burst out
laughing. "Chicken pox!"

It seemed too good to be true. If that was all, there
was nothing to get upset about.

"Chicken pox," Marty echoed. "We were really worried."

"You should be," Anne said.

"What is it?" Dad was disturbed by the slight quaver
he heard in her voice.

Anne had been dreading this moment all the way
home. "His white count is so depleted, the doctor says
there's no way his body can fight the disease."

Silence returned, and fear, a new fear this time.

"What's going to happen?" Dad asked.

"He'll probably get sores all over his body. And his
fever's going to shoot up. All they can do is try to keep
it from going too high."

"From *chicken pox?*" Michael said.

"I had chicken pox five or six years ago," Jean reminded them. "It wasn't much fun, and I remember I

had to stay in the dark for a couple of days, but it wasn't any big deal."

"It is for Joey," Anne said.

They looked at one another, sharing the same thought. To a haemophiliac, a simple cut finger can be fatal. To a child suffering from leukemia, his body already weakened and his very vitality under siege, any number of minor diseases can be serious. All of the family gathered in the secure, comfortable house—all healthy, all eager to laugh off something as inconsequential as chicken pox—suddenly had to reevaluate that common childhood disease. To an otherwise healthy child, it was a nuisance; to Joey it could be fatal.

"I think maybe we better have John come home," Dad said.

"I'll call him," Marty said. "Mom, you sit down and have something to eat."

"No, I'm fine."

"Anne?" Dad said. "Please."

She sighed and sat down. Martin went to the kitchen and picked up the phone.

The call to John was a good idea for several reasons. Whenever a problem important enough to concern the whole family arose, a solution was arrived at by family conference. It was understood by everyone that Anne and John Sr. would make any final decision, but each opinion was valuable. Each opinion affected the outcome. Now, with new danger for Joey, John's presence was necessary.

Especially John's. A special bond existed between John and Joey. John himself had always looked up to Marty, turning to him for help and approval; the bond between them was a natural one that had grown as a matter of course. But Martin no longer lived at home, and as much as Joey loved the rest of the family he had a special feeling for John. Anne knew that if John's presence could offer Joey any help in the difficulties ahead, John would be there.

By the time John got home from Penn State, Joey was in critical condition, with a temperature of 105.

John and his parents went straight to the hospital. After a few words with the duty nurse they entered Joey's darkened room. On his high hospital bed a rubber sheet had been stretched taut over a cooling ice pack. Joey, in a short hospital gown, lay uncovered and unmoving. Dwarfed by the bed, he looked even more fragile and helpless. An IV tube snaked down from a suspended bottle of glucose solution to the adhesive tape on his forearm; catheters and the electronic sensors of monitoring equipment were connected. His eyes were closed.

Dad and Anne stopped near the door. John walked closer and crouched beside the bed.

"Joey? Hey, Hoss?"

There was no response. Then Joey moved slightly and his eyes eased open. When he saw his brother leaning over him, the faintest hint of a smile crossed his lips.

John motioned his parents closer. Anne shook her head. Her husband grasped a chair and slid it quietly to John, who sat and leaned across the bed.

"Hey, look at you," he said. "They've got you on ice like a can of beer."

It was an effort but Joey found the strength to answer. "Feels good," he said, " 'cause I'm so hot." His hand scratched restlessly at the sheet. His eyes closed.

John reached down to take the small hand in his. Clasping it, he held Joey's hand tightly as if to will his own strength through that firm grip into Joey. When Joey opened his eyes a second time, John pantomimed chewing Joey's knuckle, trying to draw a grin from the boy. But Joey's eyes closed once more and he lay still.

5

"Medicine is still an inexact art," Doctor Wingreen said. "I wish I could claim otherwise. I'd like to encourage you, but I know you want to hear the truth." He stood outside the closed door of Joey's room and talked with Anne and John, Sr.

"We do," Anne said.

"What it comes down to is that Joey simply isn't producing the antibodies he needs to fight the disease. Normally, even for a small child, chicken pox is relatively harmless because the body's own immunological system fights it efficiently enough. But in Joey's case . . . Well, let's say that Joey's system is on strike. It's not working."

"What is there we can do?" asked Dad.

"Nothing very much, I'm afraid. Oh, you can be there, beside him, in case he should waken." The doctor smiled gently. "The texts don't say much about it, but I'm convinced that love and attention are better medicine than half the antibiotics I've ever prescribed." He held up a hand to ward off the objection showing in Anne's eyes. "I know, I know. You're already giving him that.

"Excuse me, I shouldn't keep you standing. Can we go sit down?"

They walked down the quiet corridor to the waiting area, talking as they went.

"There's one other possibility," Doctor Wingreen continued. "If Joey were to get a transfusion from someone who's recently recovered from a bout with chicken pox, the antibodies he needs would be present in that blood. It might be the answer we're looking for."

"Then that's it," Dad said.

"It's not so easy." Doctor Wingreen indicated a

pair of chairs. "Please. I know you two are exhausted."
He sat across from them. "We rarely if ever take blood
from a child, for a number of reasons. That means
we'll have to locate an adult donor, and the number of
adults who come down with chicken pox is pretty
small."

"But there must be some," Anne said.

"Certainly. Some. I had a patient myself no more
than two years ago—a man of thirty-five who suddenly
contracted it. How he'd reached that age without ever
having been exposed to it, I'll never know, but he
had."

"Well then, there you are," Anne persisted.

"No. I've got to repeat myself. Not only an adult,
but one who's had chicken pox within the last two
weeks. A week would be even better. And when I
say one of my patients, two years ago, well . . . I'd hate
to guess how many patients I've seen since then."

Anne looked at her husband, who nodded. When he
spoke, it was, as always, in a soft, low voice, but there
was no mistaking the authority behind the words. "We
understand. It's not common, but it does happen. How
do we go about locating the right donor?"

"I wish I could tell you that," Doctor Wingreen
said.

"A specialist!" Anne said quickly. "Isn't there a
specialist of some kind we could ask?"

Doctor Wingreen shook his head. "Colleagues in
virology, immunology, neurosurgeons—all of us, no
matter what our specialties might be, occasionally see
adult patients with childhood diseases. I've already
spoken to at least a dozen members of the hospital
staff here. We've posted notes on both bulletin boards
outside Emergency and in the Out-Patient Clinic waiting rooms. And my receptionist is checking hospital
records. I'm hoping we'll turn up just the donor we
need."

"I think we can do more than hope," Dad said.

"How?"

"There are six of us," Anne said. She got a confirming nod from her husband. "Six of us, only one of you, and you're busy. We'll find the person."

"I hope you can." Doctor Wingreen rose. "I don't mean to frighten you, but it's got to be fast."

"How fast?" Dad asked. He was on his feet too.

"I'd like to say two days, but I'm not even certain of that. Joey's stable now but he's not improving. We can bring down the fever a bit, but if we can't break it and correct the body's lack of immunity, I'm afraid two days is really all I can promise. If we locate a donor, we may have a chance, but it's got to be right now."

Anne tugged impatiently at her husband's sleeve. "We'll do it." They headed for the elevator.

"And I'll keep working on it," Doctor Wingreen called after them. "But I won't refuse any help you can offer."

They mobilized their forces. Sitting around the dining room table the Cappellettis sorted out responsibilities and made up a list. Finally, Anne read off the assignments. "Marty and Joyce use the phones. Try all the hospitals in town. See if you can find someone —a grown-up, I mean—in one of the hospitals right now with chicken pox. Mike, you and Jeannie have school and I don't want you to worry about this."

"We can miss school for one day," Michael protested. "You know you need us."

"He's right, Mom."

"Well, there probably is one way you could help. I know this may not work, but you can go through the yellow pages and start calling doctors. That's all I can think of."

Jean asked, "Will Dad be able to get off work today?"

"He won't need to," her mother said. "He's already talking to the man at union headquarters. They're going to check through the Blue Cross/Blue Shield office to see if any claims have been filed lately. Now, can anybody think of anything else?"

They sat for a moment longer. Marty said, "It doesn't

do much good to sit and worry about it. Let's get going."

Joyce and Marty left, Martin to use his home phone and Joyce to use a neighbor's. Jean and Michael went to relatives' houses to begin making their calls. "I'll take A-to-L," Jean said as she dashed out. John had returned to Penn State the night before—an exam was scheduled for this morning—but would be back by evening. Anne would serve as command-post controller; the children would check in with her, giving progress reports every few hours.

Unfortunately, they were lack-of-progress reports. And precious time was passing. By noon, phone numbers were dancing in front of their eyes, the same word—"No"—echoing and re-echoing in their ears.

Dad had spoken to the union steward, who'd been unable to help. Contact with Blue Cross and Blue Shield had also turned up no helpful information.

He was sitting over lunch at the construction site where he worked, talking with a pair of fellow workers. Roy Blaney, one of the high-walkers who assembled the steel-girder framework of large buildings, lay back with a sack of cement for a pillow, hardhat down over his eyes, hands clasped across his stomach, sympathizing.

"It's rough, John. I wish I could help, but I can't think of a thing."

The third man stared into space for a moment before he said, "Well, I had an idea that might work. I know when our Laura had an operation that time and they needed blood, they went through records of people who gave transfusions before, then they called some of them."

"No good," John said. "Thanks anyway, Tony. It's not just who's willing to give blood, or what type they've got. It has to be somebody who's had the chicken pox."

"You could always go to the radio," Roy said.

"What do you mean, 'radio'?"

"I heard it once. They had this kid who had an appendix operation or something, and he needed negative blood—you know what I mean? RH negative? So this disc jockey almost all one day, between records, he kept saying, 'If you've got RH negative such-and-such, call this number because they need your blood for an operation.' You could try something like that, John." Roy tilted the hardhat back off his eyes and sat up. "John? Where you going?"

The foreman's shack on the construction site had a telephone. That's where John was already headed.

A Philadelphia radio station agreed to carry the message periodically, including the Cappelletti phone number. The station manager couldn't promise to broadcast it regularly, nor could he give any assurance that the right person might be listening, but he was willing to make the effort.

After the first announcement, Anne wouldn't leave the phone. Thousands of people must be tuned to that station. Surely one of them would respond. She waited for over four hours.

But the phone was silent.

It was 8:30 that night when the family finally reassembled. No one had any positive results to report. Most doctors' offices were already closed, making further phone calls a waste of time. Blue Cross and Blue Shield had located no recent claims for any subscriber hospitalized because of chicken pox. Depressed, the family sat around the table, trying to think of yet another way to search for the needed donor.

It was then that the phone call came through.

A Mrs. William Frome, in a small town some thirty miles northwest of Philadelphia, had been driving her daughter home from dancing class when she heard the plea on her radio. She had called at once to offer herself as the donor.

Nineteen hours after Doctor Wingreen had defined their best hope for Joey's recovery, Dad Cappelletti sat in a folding chair outside a laboratory room at the hospital and watched Mrs. Frome emerge from the room. In the crook of her left elbow lay a gauze pad covered by a small strip of adhesive tape. She was settling a sweater around her shoulders.

"I can't tell you how much we thank you, Mrs. Frome," he said.

"I'm glad I could do it. Do you suppose I could see your son?"

After a brief hesitation, Dad said, "He's in a coma, but what you did—"

"Oh, I'm so sorry. Of course, never mind."

"But you see, what you did is going to . . ." He broke off as he saw Anne coming out of Joey's room down the corridor. As she approached, he continued: "I was just telling Mrs. Frome, we're sure he's going to be better, thanks to her."

"Yes, we do thank you so much," Anne said.

"I have a daughter his age," Mrs. Frome said. It was explanation enough. She patted Anne's hand and walked toward the elevators.

"You can go home now, Anne," Dad said. "There's no point in switching if you don't get a good night's sleep."

"Now you be sure and wake me if he—"

"Mr. and Mrs. Cappelletti!" A young intern called enthusiastically to them. He was reading a clipboard. Then, embarrassed at his own exuberance, he ducked his head.

They walked toward him.

"I was just reading your son's chart," he said. "It's remarkable, isn't it?"

"What is?" Dad asked.

"The complete remission in leukemia cells."

"Yes, they told us." Anne nodded, clearly not as excited as he was by the news.

But the intern remained fascinated. "I'm sure it's the chicken pox virus that does it."

Dad spoke carefully, his voice neutral. "Doctor Wingreen said it's only temporary."

"Well, yes. Yes, I'm sure it would be," the intern said. "But we ought to be thankful anyway." He smiled with youthful encouragement as he laid the clipboard on the counter.

Joey's parents looked first at each other, then back at the door behind which their desperately ill boy lay at that moment, a single question in their minds: why should they be thankful when Joey might well die of chicken pox, rather than leukemia? The fact that one possibly fatal disease was combatting the other was not something to make them cheerful. The scientific discovery might intrigue an intern, but it was not the sort of news that worried parents could respond to.

"Remember, call me if he makes a change." Anne kissed her husband's cheek.

"You get some rest." Dad watched her walk to the elevator, push the button, and enter when the doors opened almost immediately. She turned to smile encouragement to him. He nodded. The doors closed on her wave.

The intern, still attentive, had misunderstood their smiles. Surely the Cappellettis must have been encouraged by his enthusiasm.

"Mr. Cappelletti?" the intern said.

"Yes?"

"About your son . . ."

"He'll be okay, he'll be fine. And thanks for your interest."

The intern nodded and walked away, whistling softly to himself.

Joey's father returned to the chair in Joey's room to keep his vigil.

6

It was 2:30 a.m., the night so quiet that the horn of a semi-trailer passing on WestChester Pike several blocks from the Cappelletti home woke John from a restless sleep. For several minutes he lay staring at the ceiling in the darkness, now and then diverted by the lights of a late-night car out front throwing the shadows of bare elm branches across his ceiling.

Finally, when it became clear that sleep was no

longer possible, he rose quietly and fumbled around the room to find his slippers. Somehow, he managed to locate them without waking Michael. He walked down the steps carefully, trying not to waken anyone else. The third step from the top always squeaked, so he skipped it—one hand supporting his weight on the banister while he took the long stride over the noisy tread. He passed through the living room by feel, then through the dining room and into the kitchen.

In the refrigerator he found a bottle of ginger ale. Tucking an apple under his chin, he took out a Saran-wrapped plate of leftover chicken, intending to bump the refrigerator door shut with his hip.

"Are you hungry, Johnny?"

The voice startled him and nearly made him drop everything.

"What?" By the light of the still-open refrigerator he saw his mother seated at the dining room table.

"What are you doing there?" He snapped on the kitchen light.

She shielded her eyes from the sudden glare of light shining through the kitchen doorway and motioned him to come closer.

"I said, what are you doing sitting in the dark?"

"You walked right by me."

"I guess I was concentrating too much on this chicken." John slid the plate onto the dining table and sat down across from his mother. She was a silhouette against the bay window behind her. "Why didn't you turn on some lights?"

"Never mind. Let's just sit here."

"A problem?" John asked.

"Some thinking to do, that's all. Do you want me to fix you something more? That's not very much on your plate."

"No, no, this is fine." He polished the apple on his pajama sleeve and waited.

"I was telling your dad today," Anne said. "I'm glad, if this had to happen at all, it happened toward the end of your season. It's good to have you home so often."

"Triples your food bills though, doesn't it?"

Anne's smile was tired. "Tell me a better way to spend the money." She reached over to squeeze his hand, and they sat in silence.

"You ought to get some sleep," John told her.

"In a minute."

John held out a chicken wing, offering it, but when Anne shook her head he gnawed at the cold chicken, washing it down with ginger ale.

"Don't you think you ought to go upstairs?" he said. "After spending all day at the hospital, you can't sit up the whole night too."

"I'm fine. Besides, I took a short nap at the hospital."

"Uh-huh. I know you. Your 'nap' was thirty seconds, and then you felt guilty about even that much." When she wouldn't respond, he knew how worried she was. "I worry sometimes, Mom, about whether we do enough for Joey."

"Oh, come on now."

"I don't mean you and Dad," he said. "There's nothing more the two of you *could* do. But the rest of us—"

"Johnny, that's pure nonsense."

"Well, maybe so. But I still worry."

Anne tried to lighten his mood. "Tell you what. We'll split the work: you go to sleep, and let me do your share of the worrying."

"No, listen. Dad's down at the hospital sitting around tonight, and he's got to go to work in the morning. I know you were there all day, and you're spending the night sitting up at home. When do the two of you get any rest? We ought to do more for you."

Anne shook her head. "Jean is like a second mother to Joey. Michael never has to be asked to spend time with him—and time he ought to be spending with friends his own age. Marty comes over every night after work. Joyce is like one of the blood family."

"Uh-huh. And I'm off playing football."

"Not now you're not."

"I am most of the time."

"What's wrong with playing football, for goodness sake?"

John groped for words, unable to express his feelings. "Nothing, I guess. It's just that—"

"Johnny, God gave you special abilities. I believe that."

He looked at her but her expression was difficult to read in the half-light washing over her from the kitchen. When he spoke, pain was evident in his voice. "What did God give Joey?"

"Are you questioning?" Anne's voice was suddenly sharp.

"Sure. Of course I am. Don't you ever question?"

"No." Then, as she heard the bravado of her own statement, she sagged. "Of course I do, Johnny. For so long I've prayed that Joey would *live*. Just that, just stay alive. Now I don't even know why."

John reached out to take her hand again. "Mom."

She pulled back. Her shoulders were set in determination. "Well, I'm not going to pray that tonight."

"What do you mean?"

"I've been sitting here, thinking. It's been selfish, I know that now."

He laid the chicken wing on the plate and pushed the plate away from him, as if it interferred with their conversation. "Now you've lost me, Mom. I don't have any idea what you're talking about."

"He suffers so much, Johnny, and it's selfish of me to pray that he keep going through it."

"Well, if you—"

"So tonight I'm going to pray that Joey dies."

Stunned, John paused to let the words echo around him, to be certain he had heard his mother correctly. "Oh, come on now. You can't—"

Anne rose to her feet. "I am, Johnny. I mean it. Because, if Joey has to die, then I'm going to ask God to let him die now, so he won't have to suffer anymore."

There was nothing John could say. He reached over to pull her nearer. She stood beside him, her eyes

averted; but one hand reached out to rest on his cheek.
He waited for a response to all the questions he
couldn't express, an elaboration, a change of heart . . .
any other word.

But no more words were forthcoming. Quietly resolved, Anne turned and walked upstairs.

When John woke in the morning, the sun was bright
through his bedroom window. From downstairs he
heard the faint sounds of someone moving around in
the kitchen. He got up.

As he walked into the kitchen, Jean was pouring
orange juice. Anne seemed cheerful. She was humming, almost singing.

"You can start the toast, dear," she said.

"Okay," said Jean.

"Morning."

"Good morning, Johnny." Anne's voice was relaxed
and cheerful. "You'd better call Michael."

The lightness of her mood surprised him. He peered
closer to see whether she was assuming a cheerful
facade in order to cheer the rest of them. "You sound
like you had a good night's sleep."

"I did."

John shook his head with wonder. When he'd last
seen her . . . He turned and yelled back. "Mike, roll
out!" Then he said, "I was a little worried about you
last night."

"Because of what I said?" Anne asked. "Oh, Jeannie, hand me one of those paper towels."

"Here. What did you say?"

"That I was going to pray for Joey to die." Anne
calmly turned a few pieces of sizzling bacon with her
fork.

"Mom! You didn't!" Jean nearly dropped the toast
she was buttering.

"I did."

"You did *what?*" Jean asked, glancing at John in
bewilderment. "You really said that, or . . . you really
prayed for that?"

Anne's tone of voice was as matter-of-fact as if she were describing what she'd eaten for lunch the day before. "I prayed," she said. "And I got an answer." She spread the paper towel on the stove top and laid a piece of bacon on it to drain.

John was nearly afraid to ask. "What kind of answer?"

"There was . . . well, I don't know how to describe it. A presence, I guess. A presence in my room." She glanced at her children. "And you can both smile, if you want to."

Neither was smiling. "What happened, Mom?" John asked.

"I was told, Joey's not going to die."

The children exchanged glances, not really certain how to take the comment.

"He's going to survive this crisis," Anne said confidently.

"You sound awfully sure," Jean said.

"I am. Now will you eat your breakfast? That toast is going to get cold." She turned back to the skillet and drew out another strip of bacon, humming again.

7

"Frankly, I don't have much confidence that Joey will regain consciousness." Doctor Wingreen sat at a table in the hospital conference room and toyed with a Styrofoam coffee cup. His experience had taught him that the truth, direct and immediate, was always better than any mistaken notion of sparing his patients. But he hated telling them. It was times like this that found him repeating a useless habit: the fingers of one hand reached up to rake through his hair. He had been nearly bald for several years.

"Do you mean . . . ?" Anne couldn't say aloud what she was thinking. And fearing.

"I mean, *ever*." His hand crushed the coffee cup and he looked at it in surprise.

The conference room was on the first floor of the hospital. A few pieces of calendar art hung on the walls—someone's attempt to brighten the room and make it less institutional. But nothing could be done to disguise the Formica-topped table and functional chairs. John sat hipshot on one corner of the table, Mike and Jean seated beside him. Joyce and Marty stood beside Anne. John Sr. rested a hand on his wife's shoulder as she toyed with the handbag in her lap.

"Are you sure?" he asked.

"There's no way to be absolutely certain," Doctor Wingreen admitted. "But we do have some indicators. His temperature's been down long enough and he's still in the coma. We should have had more positive response by now."

"Do you know *why* he hasn't come out of it?" asked Marty.

"We can't discount the possibility of brain damage." The doctor looked from one anxious face to another, trying to make certain that they all understood what he was saying. He knew his tendency in painful conferences like this was to back away from his initial assertion, if only to comfort the people who were already denying—in their own minds—what he had told them. "When the body bakes for that long, there has to be some effect."

He paused until he saw their nods of acceptance. A shift from factual information to advice was marked by the lightening of his voice. "I can't tell you what to do, of course, but I can tell you what I'd do."

"Go ahead, Doctor," Dad said.

"I'd put him in a home."

"A home!" Jean was aghast.

"Yes, I can imagine what that idea does to you, but you really ought to consider it." Again the doctor brushed a palm over his scalp. "I know it's a big step."

"What could they do for him in a home that we can't do ourselves?" asked Michael.

"That's not really the point. The point is that nobody can do anything for him. And look at it this way: your family's been through enough."

John rose. "You said you weren't sure. He might come out of it."

The doctor wouldn't let them take that easy out. "What I said was, I couldn't swear he won't, but I really don't believe there's a chance."

"But you're not certain," Anne persisted.

The doctor continued his explanation. He tried to sway them to his point of view, choosing the kindest words possible to explain what was, after all, the sort of situation no one wants to be told about. He scanned the faces watching him as he spoke, but reluctance was all he saw wherever he looked. Finally he said, "Maybe you youngsters wouldn't mind leaving the room. Give your mother and father the chance to discuss this."

"If we wanted it that way, Anne and I would have come down here alone," Dad said.

"That's true, Doctor," Anne said. "We asked the children to be with us because it's their decision as well."

"Surely you don't mean that. It's you two who will—"

"We mean it," Dad said.

"Very well." Doctor Wingreen leaned back in his chair, waiting. "That's all I can say."

There was a moment of silence while Dad took a tally of the expressions visible. "What do you think?" he asked them.

"I think he should be at home," John said.

"Yes," said Jean.

"I do too," Michael agreed quickly.

Marty and Joyce nodded their agreement.

Doctor Wingreen turned away from the parents to focus his argument on the children. "I understand how you feel, believe me. But are you considering what it's going to be like for your mother?"

"Now there's no need to worry about me." Anne's voice was strong, her smile confident.

Joyce spoke to her mother-in-law, ignoring the doctor. "Marty and I can come over at night and relieve you."

"Sure," Marty said.

"And I'll be home on weekends," John told them. "I can take over then."

"We'll put his bed in the dining room." Jean was on her feet now, her eyes shining as the family planning took shape. "That way you won't have to be running up and down stairs."

Doctor Wingreen shook his head in disbelief. The faces he saw now were brighter and happier—as if their commitment to a common plan had solved all their problems. But he was convinced that their commitment, no matter how heartfelt, couldn't change the basic facts of Joey's condition.

"We know you'll all help," Dad said.

Anne looked at each of her children, one at a time, returning the nods she got in turn. Then she turned to the doctor. "Well . . ."

With a small shrug, Doctor Wingreen rose. "I still think it's a bad idea, but I can see I'm outnumbered."

"Doctor, we appreciate your advice," Dad told him. "But it is our decision, and it looks like we made it."

The dining room became a hospital room, and a less institutional and cheerier one than most. A leaf was removed from the large maple table to make it smaller, two of the chairs were moved to the den behind the kitchen, and in the extra space provided a hospital bed was placed, beside the big bay window through which sunlight streamed into the room every morning. It was higher than the usual bed, the mattress a full foot farther from the floor, and adjustable.

On it lay the pale, motionless figure of Joey. Beside the bed stood the rack which held a bottle and the tube periodically inserted through Joey's nostril to provide nourishment, his liquid meals. Scotch-taped to the wall above the bed were get-well cards from friends and relatives. Their colorful messages cheered the rest of the family more than they did Joey. Still in his coma, he wasn't even aware of them.

The Christmas holidays were not the joyous occasions they had always been in the past, but neither were they gloomy. Without his knowing it, Joey was included in all the activities. Dinnertimes still had their share of happy banter. And dinner on Christmas Eve —a tradition that Anne Cappelletti was especially proud of—was particularly festive.

She and Jean spent the day preparing special dishes. The warm kitchen was fragrant now with the mingled scents of rosemary and oregano. The meal was known as the Cappelletti "fish dinner," though that term did no real justice to the feast that covered the dining-room table: soup, pasta, a favorite green salad, butter-drenched sweet potatoes and corn, and the dish Anne was most proud of, anchovies dipped in batter and deep-fried.

Before sitting down to eat, Michael went outside with a treat for the family's two cats. That, too, was a Christmas tradition in the Cappelletti home: to feed the animals before the family ate—a commemorative gesture for the animals that had shared their stable with the infant Jesus on the first Christmas Eve.

Then they gathered around the table, where they sampled every course, though in fact it was Anne and John Sr. who ended up eating most of the food. The others tried a bit of this, a little of that. And as they ate, they took turns sitting at Joey's bedside to include him in their celebration.

Later, clearing the table, Anne thought back over some of the past Christmases spent in this house, since they'd bought it twenty years ago: a first Christmas was celebrated here for each of the children but Martin, born before they'd moved to Upper Darby. One year dinner had burned to a cinder, with guests expected, and there was much confusion as her husband helped her put another together, a nearly "instant" meal.

They had established a silly tradition—she couldn't recall how it had started. Every year each child was

allowed to open a single gift on Christmas Eve, saving
the rest till Christmas morning. One year there was a
coincidence: both Martin and John had opened the
squirt-guns they'd been given. On every Christmas
Eve thereafter, until the boys got too old, each of
them opened a single, small package, for each of
them a new squirt-gun. They made Christmas morning
a pitched battle in the Cappelletti home—the boys
running amok in the midst of torn wrapping paper and
ribbon, shouting and laughing as they squirted hand-
sized blots on each other's shirts, as Anne circulated
among them carrying a plate of almond paste cookies
dotted with pignoli—pine nuts—on top. Dad sat in his
corner chair, threatening never again to give squirt-
guns as gifts but taking secret delight in the chaos.
And each year new squirt-guns appeared. Anne looked
again under the tree at the small package for Joey—
the squirt-gun he wouldn't be able to open.

With all those memories enriching her evening, Anne
couldn't feel altogether depressed about her youngest
son: though he wasn't an active part of the celebration,
he was there, and the family was together once again.

Throughout the holiday week, friends and relatives
stopped in and the Cappellettis made their own visits
to neighbors. But one of them always remained at
home to keep Joey company and see to his needs. And
as the holiday season passed, it almost seemed as though
nothing had changed in their lives, as if Joey were
only sleeping and would awaken soon. They all held
in common the same quiet confidence: surely time and
their collective efforts would bring Joey back to them.

SPRING 1972

8

As late winter became early spring in University Park, it was the "cold term"—skiing on Mt. Nittany and ice skating on frozen ponds and streams. Students hurried through the freezing winds from one class to the next, cheeks red and hands chapped.

In Upper Darby at the Cappelletti house, the term was called the "good one." John, no longer so busy with football practice and games, got to come home more often.

One March weekend found him sprawled on the floor in his stocking feet in front of the living-room fireplace, a book propped up between him and the flickering flames. His father sat in his overstuffed chair, jotting figures on a long yellow pad. It was time to begin figuring his income taxes.

"John, you'll strain your eyes, reading in that light," his father said.

Anne brought in a plate of sliced cheese. "Is that any way to talk to one of your dependents?" she asked, winking at John. "Here. Have a snack."

John rolled onto his elbow. "Any potato chips?"

"You and that junk food," Anne said.

"Gotta keep up my strength."

"Cheese is good for you." She held the plate lower for John to help himself. When he hesitated, head cocked, she laughed and said, "Okay. There's a soda in the refrigerator."

"Root beer?"

"Don't get fussy now, or you can get it yourself." She handed him the plate and left to get the soda.

"Hey, dependent," Dad said. John held out the plate and his father helped himself.

It was a relaxing evening. John played a game of

gin rummy with Michael, took a few minutes to help Jean with her homework, and spent half an hour sitting with Joey, talking quietly to the unresponsive boy, massaging his arms and legs.

"Have to leave early?" Dad asked, as John started up the stairs.

"My first class isn't till noon. I'll get there okay."

"Nice having you home, John."

"Me too. It recharges my batteries." He smiled at his father, neither of them able to verbalize more than that, though both were aware of how much more they meant. "Good night. G'nite, Mom!"

Next morning, his mother was seeing him off. "I put your shirts in your closet," she said.

"I got them." He patted the suitcase and set it down beside the front door.

"Don't forget to tell Joey good-bye."

John nodded. Hiking a chair up next to Joey's bed, John looked down at his brother. "Well, Hoss. I'm off."

There was no response. Somehow, this morning, it was unusually difficult for John to carry on a one-sided conversation. "I won't be seeing you for a while. It'll be spring practice before I get back here, the way things look now."

John ached for an answer, for some sign that Joey knew the feelings he was trying to express. "Well, you hang in there, okay?"

Still no response. Joey lay motionless, his face pale, his eyes closed. His hair was longer now, and lank, spread out on the pillow under his neck. His whole body was flaccid. John's heart was aching, his throat tightening. He couldn't bring himself to say anything more.

At spring practice that year, Coach Paterno moved John to offense. His sophomore year at defensive back had been only temporary—something the other Cappellettis had assumed, though John himself hadn't been as confident as his family. But with Lydell Mitchell and Franco Harris carrying the ball, there'd been no room for John to work into the offensive backfield. Too good an athelete to have his talents wasted, he'd been made a defensive back out of necessity. Now he was back where he belonged. All he had to do was make his position secure.

Penn State had big shoes to fill at tailback—before Mitchell, the brilliant Lenny Moore had run out of that spot—and John knew how much he had to accomplish to replace names like that in Paterno's famed running attack. He had no hope at all of replacing them in the fans' estimation, but he worked as hard as he ever had in his life, trying to fit into an already functioning backfield unit. It meant hours of fatiguing drills and bone-jarring scrimmages, with Paterno and backfield coach Bob Phillips beside him, patiently explaining what they expected of him. There was the offensive system to learn, with all the physical exercise, stretching out muscles gone tight over the winter layoff, and getting his timing down. John learned and improved daily.

And when spring practice ended it was clear that he had won the job. But in addition to the hours demanded by football, John had his classes to worry about—and Joey. If the weeks passed slowly for John, no time at all had passed for his youngest brother, who still lay motionless in bed. With these concerns on his mind, John seized the opportunity for a ride back home with a friend who was driving to Philadelphia. After class that morning, he threw textbooks and bag into the back seat of his friend's car. They split driving duties on the way home.

Anne was in the kitchen when the front door banged open.

"Anybody want to buy some dirty laundry?"

"Johnny!" She ran to meet him. She gave him a fierce hug.

John laughed. "Hey! Hey! Let me get my breath, will you?"

Michael clattered down the stairs. "Hey, man, what are you doing home?"

"What do you say?" John shook Mike's hand.

"Johnny!" Anne said. "What's the matter with your nose?"

John ignored his mother's question.

"Aren't you in school these days?" he asked Michael.

"Teachers' convention, or something. We got the afternoon off."

"John? I asked you a question."

"This?" He fingered a scab on the bridge of his nose. "Oh, a linebacker hit me, that's all."

"Doesn't it hurt?"

"Sure it hurts!"

"Oops, my sauce is burning!" She hurried to the kitchen, calling out. "It's going to leave a scar, you know that?" And then: "Say hello to Joey."

Michael canted his head toward the kitchen and shrugged. Then the two of them walked to the bed beneath the large window. Joey looked exactly as he had when John had last seen him—perhaps a bit paler, perhaps even thinner, but still motionless.

"Talk to him," Michael said quietly.

"Can he hear me?" John asked.

"No, he can't," Michael said. "But it matters to her." He pointed toward the kitchen.

"Joey!" Anne called. "Isn't it nice to have Johnny home?"

Michael nodded. "What did I tell you?"

"I wouldn't want it any other way."

"I'm with you." Michael thumped John on the shoulder. "Talk later? I've got some school work waiting for me."

John smiled good-bye and turned back to Joey. "How's it going, Hoss?"

"I asked Marty and Joyce to have dinner with us tonight," Anne called.

"It'll be good to see them."

"Don't you think Joey looks better?"

"Sure, Mom. He looks . . . fine." John reached down to knead Joey's frail arm gently.

"I told him this morning I thought he had more color in his face than I've seen in a long time."

John nodded. Then he spoke to Joey, his words really intended for his mother's ear. "Well, Hoss, looks like I'm going to get to carry the ball next season. Coach says I'm never going to be an Olympic sprinter, but I'm pretty stubborn when I'm on my feet." He squinted, his attention caught by a slight movement of the frail body glimpsed out of the corner of his eye. "Mom? Has he moved at all?" When there was no answer he called again, louder. *"Mom!"*

She was standing behind him, though he'd been too intent on Joey to see her enter the room. Slowly this time, fighting the discouragement the weeks of Joey's coma had forced on her, she said, "I heard you, John. No, he hasn't; but he will."

John spoke without turning. "Look here."

"What?"

"Look!" He pointed at Joey's open hand, lying on the bed.

The boy's face was still a mask. But his hand had begun to move almost imperceptibly. His weakened fingers clenched into a loose little fist, opened and closed again.

"Has he done that before?" John asked.

"No, he hasn't. It's the first move he's made in I don't know how long." Anne laid a hand on John's cheek. "It's having you here that does it. I'm so glad you came home."

"Me, nothing," John laughed. "It's that sauce he smells cooking in the kitchen."

They grinned at each other and turned back to look at Joey's fist. Again it opened and closed.

That small movement wasn't much, but it was a start, a hopeful sign. John and his mother stood there shaken, sharing their gratitude for the boundless possibilities implied by the life in Joey's hand.

9

Soon there was increased movement, more and more each day.

Still unable to talk, Joey lay on his bed and soaked up impressions. For most of the daytime he was awake—and alert. Cars passing by on the street outside drew his attention. And when the weather warmed and the window beside his bed was opened, his interested dark eyes followed the flash of cardinals and bluejays alighting on the feeder his father had hung outside the window. Yellow branches of forsythia waved, graceful in the spring breeze, and the lush scent of lilac drifted into the room.

John was back at school most of that spring semester, but the rest of the family spent many long hours working with Joey. Jean came home from school and held his hand, talking to him, trying to get his attention. Although he usually remained unresponsive, his eyes unfocused like a baby's, he was apparently content, if not the old Joey they knew. He was like a new member of the family. He recognized no one, he said nothing, and, like an infant, he seemed to have everything to learn.

Anne brought his meals and fed him. From time to time she remarked on her feelings to her husband. "It's funny," she told him, "having an eighty-pound baby in the house. A strange feeling."

"A good feeling," Dad said.

"Maybe it's just that it's hard for me to think of starting a new family." She spooned carrots from the bowl and held them to Joey's lips. He ate, his eyes following the spoon and glancing quickly aside at any sudden motion in the room.

Most of the time his condition cheered them. He was

healthy and in no apparent pain. They had moments of depression as well, of impatience at the rate of Joey's recovery. But there was some comfort in recognizing that Joey's condition wasn't unique. Other families have been through similar experiences. Adult stroke victims often revert to a childlike state, and seem to need constant attention. And post-convulsion reversion to earliest childhood isn't uncommon in young children.

Marty and Michael sat beside Joey's bed, holding his hands and "patterning" him. His muscular coordination was poor and he needed the exercise. They would take the boy's hands and move them alternately, extending and pushing the arms back in a cycle like moving the pedals of a bicycle. Then they did the same thing with his legs.

The exercise was more than merely physical. For psychologists have discovered that adults who have reading difficulties, or who stammer, share an early experience. During childhood they skip a step in the normal development most children undergo. They bypass crawling and go directly from creeping, or hunching themselves along the floor, to walking. Crawling— the alternation of right hand, left hand, right leg, left leg—helps to "pattern" the brain, and gives a child the ability to distinguish left from right.

What Marty and Michael did was what any physiotherapist might have done. They established the distinction between left and right and prepared the boy for the development of language skills. And in a few weeks Joey's coordination developed rapidly—much more rapidly than a baby's. He was, after all, nine years old; and he wasn't so much learning new skills as he was relearning skills forgotten. In those few weeks he made the progress of many months.

Joey also learned fast because he had a houseful of loving people to help him. And soon his recognition of each of them was marked by smiles as they passed his bed or spoke softly to him. But still he was silent, still he didn't speak.

Each morning on his way out of the house to go to work, Dad stopped to talk for a moment before leaving. "You have a good day now, Joey," he'd say.

Smiling, Joey would glance from his father to the window beside him, his eyes roving, his face cheerful.

"I'll see you tonight." Dad would lean over to pat Joey's shoulder.

And in the evening at dinnertime the family continued to include their youngest member in the conversation. Without really responding, Joey seemed to enjoy these times. After dinner someone usually sat and played games with him. They tried to get him to recognize objects they held up and named . . . a book, a toy truck, an apple.

And then, one night after Joyce and Marty had joined the family for dinner and everyone had gathered later at Joey's bed, it happened.

"Tell me what this is, Joey." Marty held up a colorful rubber ball. "Come on, you can say it. This is a 'ball.' "

"He looks a lot better, don't you think?" Joyce said. "He's been putting on some weight."

Marty nodded. "When the weather gets a little warmer, we'll rig a chair or something for him to lie on, and he can get out in the sunshine."

Anne leaned over the bed. "Hear that, Joey? They're talking about you. Are you going to let them plan your future without an argument?"

"Mom," Joey said.

It was like a bombshell. Every head turned to look in astonishment at Joey. Anne dropped to her knees and seized his hand in her own. "Joey, what did you say?"

"Mom."

Everyone laughed and gathered closer around the bed. Michael touseled Joey's hair as the family chattered in happiness and relief. Anne drew her eighty-pound baby into a fierce, protective hug.

That single word marked a breakthrough. Not only was Joey's weight increasing; his strength was up, and he was more and more alert. As if speaking for the first time had been a key, Joey improved rapidly. Unlike a baby, he didn't have to learn everything from scratch; he had only to remember. And his memory returned with startling speed.

His father brought in a wheelchair and Joey was finally able to leave his bed, to sit in the chair and be moved around the house. And it wasn't long till the other Cappellettis were wishing they could turn off Joey's switch. He talked incessantly. He wanted to know the name of everything.

One Saturday evening Joyce and Jean were washing up the dinner dishes while Anne took time to relax with the newspaper. Joey sat in the kitchen, beside the refrigerator and out of the way of his sisters.

He spoke with just a hint of difficulty, the words slurred and his articulation hesitant as well as fuzzy. He paused in the midst of sentences as if searching his mind for the needed word. "What's that?" he asked, pointing.

Jean held up a bar of soap. "It's the soap, I told you."

"What do you do with it?"

Joyce turned back to the sink. "You cut your fingernails with it."

Laughing at the game they played, Joey said, "You do not."

"Then what *do* you do?" Jean asked. She carried the dried dishes from the rack beside the sink to the cupboard and stacked them neatly.

"Where's John?" Joey asked.

"Oh no you don't." Jean turned to him. "Don't put us off, now."

"Where's John?" he asked again.

Joyce said, "He's at school. Now, what do you do with the soap?"

Joey looked from one to the other, slyly. "You . . . *eat* it?" He waited for the reaction.

"Right," Joyce said, matter-of-factly. "With chocolate sauce."

"No, you don't." Joey laughed. "You don't eat it. It's *soap!*"

Unable to resist his delight, Jean reached over to tickle him.

In a few months, the old baby became Joey again— and no one was more surprised than his doctors. Anne took him to the hospital where he underwent a battery of tests, neurological examinations particularly. His coordination was a bit impaired but in other ways his responses were normal for a child of his age. In those few months Joey had grown from a helpless infant to a functioning boy of nine.

And though that fact amazed his doctors, Joey's family wasn't at all surprised. They had expected nothing less. After all, they had given him all the love and attention they had, immeasurably more than a physical therapist or even a team of nurses might have been able to give. Taking Joey home with them had been the right thing to do. There was no question in any of their minds about it. Doctor Win- green's half-joking prescription had proven effective: in some circumstances, there are better medicines than antibiotics.

With summer coming on, the school term over, John insisted on being home. He wanted to be able to help with Joey. And when he discovered that jobs were scarce in the neighborhood, he went into business for himself.

John and his father spent one weekend in the back yard working with two-by-fours, sheets of plywood and fiberboard, a power saw, and bolts, a hammer and nails. Joey sat near them in his chair, watching and badgering them with questions.

"What is it?"

"Lumber," his father said.

"But when you get done cutting it, what'll it be?"

"Cut lumber," John told him.

"Aww, c'mon, John. You can tell me."

"Nope. We'll show you."

They built a two-by-four framework, covered it with

plywood, and when they had finished they stood there admiring a small box-like shed. On one side, a hinged panel swung up as an awning over a counter area.

"A stand to sell something," Joey guessed.

"You got it, Hoss."

"Hot dogs?"

"In hot weather?" John asked. "Who wants to buy hot dogs in hot weather?"

"Okay," Joey said. *"Cold* dogs!"

John made a lunge for his brother. "Look out, there! I didn't work up a sweat like this to stand and listen to bad jokes."

"Dad! Dad! Help!" Joey called through his laughter while John tickled him.

Their father shook his head at their horseplay. Then, with a smile, he began packing away his tools.

John arranged with a friend who owned a gas station on WestChester Pike some three blocks away to let him put the stand there for the summer. And he went into business. Inside his "store," a small machine shaved and ground block ice into glistening granules; John scooped the ice into a paper cone and then let brightly colored fruit flavoring dribble over the ice.

He did a pretty good business, too. Joey sat beside him, while they listened to a portable radio and talked. They served neighborhood children on bicycles and adults too, headed for the park and playground across the street. Week after week, in good weather, they were able to be together.

Occasionally Jean spelled them, or Michael did, coming by for an hour or so in order that John and Joey could go home for meals, John pushing Joey's wheelchair ahead of him. After lunch they returned to the stand to spend the afternoon "loafing," as John called it; "having fun," according to Joey.

One morning, on their way to open the stand for the day, they walked along a tree-shaded street. Joey was in his wheelchair; John was pushing him, dressed comfortably in shorts, T-shirt and sandals. They were arguing.

"I am not," Joey said.

"Don't you know you're not supposed to argue with big brothers?"

"Even if the big brother's a turkey?" Joey's speech was normal now, the slurring and hesitation gone.

"You're really asking for it," John said. "Right into a tree . . . *pow!*" He swung the chair to one side and feinted at a tree.

"You're not a turkey, John. You're not!" Joey laughed deliriously.

John swerved back onto the sidewalk. "Wow! Just in time. You better watch what you say there, Hoss, or you're going to get mangled."

"You're not a turkey, John. You're a yo-yo!"

"That did it!" John faked a pass at another tree, shaking the chair from side to side while Joey hung on shouting. They slowed, then, and the chair bounced lightly over cracks in the sidewalk. "Now I forgot what we were talking about," John said.

Reminded and indignant, Joey looked back over his shoulder to complain, "You said I was lazy!"

"Well, you are." John thumped Joey on the head. "I wish I had someone to push me around like a potentate."

"I'll push you."

"Yeah, sure." Sorry he'd been steered into such a conversation and worried about hurting Joey's feelings, John pointed across the street and said, "How do you like the new Corvette Wilcox got?"

Joey didn't even glance at the bright-red sports car, gleaming in the sunshine. "I will, John, really. I can do it."

"Do what?"

"Aw, John, you're not even listening. I said, I'll push you."

"No gimpy little kid's going to take my job away from me."

"Come on, John. *Please?* Let me try."

John kept his face a mask, trying not to let Joey read his thoughts. He stopped the chair and bent down to kneel beside it. "You really think you're ready?"

"Sure."

"Well, I still think you're a lot of hot air, but you can try if you want to."

John stood in front of the chair and helped Joey to rise. Although the boy's speech was clearer now, other evidence of his long coma remained: his coordination was extremely poor and he moved with great caution—like someone climbing from a hospital bed uncertain of his strength and frightened of what he might discover. Joey moved one foot, then the other, sliding them over the sidewalk and leaning against John's strong hands for support till he reached the handgrip back of the chair. Joey grabbed the grip for support and held himself wavering but upright.

"Now *you* get in the chair," he said.

"What do you say you try it empty, first?"

"Come on, John. You said."

"No, no, I don't mean it like that. It'll be easier. Try it with no weight in the chair."

"Don't be afraid, I won't hurt you."

John debated a moment, then sighed and sat in the chair. "Okay, but I sure hope you know how to fly this thing."

"Just watch." Joey edged forward with his right foot, then his left. Very slowly, the chair began to roll.

"Hey! I love it!" John leaned back and crossed his long legs, laughing.

The chair gathered speed and Joey was forced to shuffle faster. He couldn't keep up with the momentum of the laden chair and it bounced away from him to roll down the sidewalk. Joey went crashing to the ground. John leaped from the chair, overturning it, and rushed back in alarm to kneel beside the fallen child.

"Are you all right?"

Joey lay on the sidewalk, his eyes closed. When he turned and lifted his head, a huge grin blossomed on his face. "What do you mean, all right? That was my imitation of you carrying the football."

John collapsed in relief, flopping down to sit on the sidewalk beside his brother. "I'm going to put you up for the Heisman Trophy," he said.

"What's the Heisman Trophy?"

"And you call yourself a football fan! It's not possible! I thought everyone knew about—"

"Aww, John, just tell me."

"It's the award they give the best college football player in the country."

"In that case," Joey said, "I'd better practice." He held out his hand. "Want to help me up?"

John got up. "See? Mention someone for the Heisman and right away he expects everybody to wait on him, hand and foot." Winking, he reached down to take Joey's hand.

Joey pulled himself up, arms trembling. John offered support but let the boy do much of the work himself.

"That's a good grip you got there, Hoss." John squeezed Joey's hand once, then slowly released it and watched Joey balance tentatively on his feet. "Maybe we'll start selling orange juice at the stand. With all those muscles, you can squeeze the oranges."

Joey smiled with pride at the camouflaged praise. Then impulsively he leaned forward, his face turned up to watch John's, and fell against his solid, stocky brother, his arms reaching out to circle John's waist in a hug. His face shone with loving pride. John reached down and pressed the boy to him, forcing a tight smile in response. He had to turn away from the spotlight of Joey's gaze when his welling eyes blurred.

10

Summer was almost over.

On the August Sunday before John had to return to

Penn State and football training camp, the entire family gathered in the back yard for a cookout. A shower the night before had brightened the lawn and creeper roses on the trellis beside the garage were fresh-rinsed pink against the white siding.

Jean and Marty were tossing horseshoes. Dad sat in a redwood lounger, leafing idly through the Sunday *Bulletin*. Anne spread a cloth over the picnic table. Then she moved a portable radio from the table to set it beside her husband's chair. Broadcaster Richie Ashburn was calling the play-by-play action of the Phillies' game. Joyce appeared with a tray of hot-dog rolls and relishes.

Marty, who'd volunteered to man the barbeque grill only if he didn't have to wear the apron his mother offered him, was pleading with her to hurry. "Joyce? Another minute and we'll be eating charcoal. Would you bring the buns over here?"

Joyce detoured past Marty to deposit the plate of rolls, then went to the table with her tray.

"Michael, Jean, get your hands washed," Anne called. "And see if you can find the Two Musketeers."

"All present and accounted for," John said. He hurried from the house, carrying Joey in his arms.

"Time to eat," their mother said.

"In a minute. First . . . *ta-dahhhh!*" John looked around the yard. "Attention everyone, the entertainment's here!"

"Yeah, watch," Joey said. His excitement was apparent.

John mimicked a stagey, announcer's voice. "I want to show you this terrific trick I taught my trained monkey." He stood Joey on his feet and shook him lightly.

Everyone laughed.

"Don't tell me you taught him how to sing," Michael said.

Jean laughed. "*John* taught him? That would be like an ostrich teaching someone how to fly."

"Hey, come on now." John feigned hurt feelings. "Why are you picking on the ringmaster?"

"They've all heard you singing," Anne said.

"Quiet! I told you, this trick takes lots of concentration." He held Joey upright, his strong hands squeezing Joey's shoulders to brace him erect. Certain that Joey had his balance, John backed slowly toward the picnic table till he was a full ten feet away from his brother. Then he called out, "Ready, Monkey?"

Joey grinned. "Ready."

"Okay." John turned to bow left and right. *Ladies* and *gentlemen . . . and Michael."*

"Hey, come on, John!"

Grinning at Michael, John said, "This trick is called . . . *walking!"*

Anne and John Sr. were puzzled for a moment before the meaning of the word sank in. Everyone was watching Joey. Very cautiously, he began to shuffle across the yard toward his brother. His head down, he observed his own clumsy feet as though they might have belonged to somebody else—first one, then the other, in slow and shaky alternation. Meanwhile, his arms were extended wide, like the wings of a bird, to help him maintain his balance.

Slowly, without taking his eyes off his son, Dad reached down to turn off the radio, fearful of any distraction. Everyone was so quiet that for the first time bird noises from the feeder out front could be heard.

Joey took a second small step, then a third. He still hadn't fallen. Then, his family watching his every move, he seemed to be gaining confidence. His steps were bolder, almost giant steps, until suddenly he was there. He fell into his brother's outstretched arms.

"Hey! Let's hear it for the monkey!" Marty shouted.

A loud cheer burst from the others, overlaid by the shrill blast of Michael's whistle that had Jean ducking in mock pain, hands clapped over her ears. For no reason she could explain, Joyce walked to Martin and put her arm around his waist to lean against him.

Anne knelt down to Joey and hugged him tightly. Her eyes were glistening.

"Terrific!" Dad rose from his chair. "Where'd you pick up this trick?"

"John and I worked on it," Joey said proudly.

"When?"

John smiled. "You didn't really think we were selling snow-cones all that time, did you?"

"I knew there was some reason you weren't making much money," Dad said.

Joey whistled for attention. "You know something else, Dad?"

"What?"

"Next summer I'm going to play Pee Wee League baseball."

Anne and Dad exchanged a worried glance. Would there, in fact, even be a next summer for Joey? But it was not the time to dwell on such thoughts, not with the joy that filled the back yard.

"As long as I get you on my team, Buster." John Sr. walked over to Joey and hugged him. Anne had turned back to the table, ostensibly to straighten the table-cloth. She was brushing the back of her hand across her eyes.

That night after Marty and Joyce had gone home and Joey had been put to bed, Anne helped John Jr. pack his suitcase. They were talking quietly.

"I'll try to make it home at least once before the football season starts."

"I'd rather you stayed at school, Johnny."

"Don't want me underfoot, is that it?"

"Now, you know better than that. I want you to concentrate on your studies." Anne held up a pair of black loafers. "Do you want to take these?"

John shook his head. "Leave 'em. And I know you were kidding about me coming home."

"For the next four months, you just worry about making good grades, and winning every game."

In mock amazement, he fell back on the bed. "Every game? Is that all?"

"Every game." Anne took his hand to pull him to his feet. "Johnny, he loves you so much, there's nothing you could do better for him than just make him proud of you." She turned away to lay the last two shirts in the suitcase before closing it.

John was unable to voice the proper response. There was nothing he wouldn't do for Joey: he was certain his mother knew that. He also felt that she was right about his not being needed at home. It would be much better for him to concentrate on a contribution to Joey's happiness that the others couldn't make. Everyone knew how Joey seemed to live for the Penn State football games.

After Joey's success at learning to walk all over again, it was now John's turn to repay his fierce determination. Joey was equally determined that John would start every game—and it was a possibility—if he didn't get injured during the season. Blinded by his hero worship, the boy almost casually expected his older brother to break records every time he stepped onto the field. John knew he had to make the effort, but he had no hope of fulfilling Joey's exaggerated expectations. Still, Joey had given him an unmistakable challenge. And what concentration and hard work could accomplish, John would do. The results would have to speak for themselves.

FALL 1972

11

That fall, Joey was assigned to special classes for the neurologically impaired. Each morning a school bus called for him at his house. Joey was not ecstatic about the arrangement. He would come out of the house to sit on the front steps, waiting glumly for the bus, his schoolbooks piled beside him. Kids he used to be friends with passed the house on their way to the near-by school where Joey had been their classmate the preceding year. They shouted and called hello to him. But if Joey answered at all, it was with a half-hearted wave. He hated to watch them going off to games he knew and teachers he'd come to like. Except for the illness he didn't even understand, he could have been sharing their good times.

His mother came out to sit on the steps beside him. She nudged him. Joey paid no attention.

"Joey, how you doin'?" two boys called from the sidewalk. "Boy, are you lucky you don't have old Whittaker this year. Look at the homework!" One of the boys waved a fistful of crumpled notepaper.

"Lucky?" Joey muttered under his breath.

"Joey," Anne whispered, "you can at least say hello."

But Joey only nodded. Then the yellow Chevy van drove up to the curb and stopped. Joey sighed, got to his feet and walked slowly toward the bus.

When he reached the open door, he turned back to call to his mother: "As far as I'm concerned, there's only one day in the week worth a darn! And that's Saturday!" He climbed into the van, slamming the door behind him.

Saturday was worth a darn because of John and Penn State. John found his spot at tailback. What's more, the Penn State fans had begun to expect excitement whenever Number 22 carried the ball.

The season opener had been disappointing to the Lion fans, their team had met a tough opponent in Tennessee—a nationally ranked team with one game already behind it on the season. The Tennessee Vols came into their match with Penn State having just enough edge in experience to take advantage of some first-half Lion jitters and jump to a 21-0 lead. It didn't take long in the second half for Penn State to find its offense, but the tide turned too late and the Lions came up short in a 28-21 loss.

But their own home opener found them ready, and the first touchdown at Beaver Stadium in the fall of '72 was scored by John Cappelletti, who bulled over from the two-yard line. He added another only minutes later, opening his own hole over right guard and taking the ball in from the one on plain determination. His second touchdown of the quarter put Penn State on top to stay for the afternoon. And when he scrambled to his feet in the end zone—untangling himself from the three defensive players who had thought they'd stopped him at the line of scrimmage, the defenders looked at him with a curious respect, as if to say 'who's the new kid?'

The game ended Penn State 21, Navy 10, and the Middies went back to Annapolis talking about John Cappelletti.

Against Iowa the following week the Nittany Lions continued their lethargic first-half play—apparently unable to generate an offense early in any game. They demonstrated another developing pattern as well: the first Penn State touchdown of the day belonged to John, a squirming, seven-yard driving run that came only in the fourth quarter. But it gave Penn State the lead. Then Iowa scored. And when quarterback John Hufnagel passed ten yards to Dan Natale for another score with only 36 seconds remaining, the Lions pulled out a squeaker, 14-10.

The Penn State offense exploded against the Illini and buried them 35-17. John Cappelletti led the way. He scored only once, on a beautiful 53-yard run, but he ran for more than a hundred yards—in the first of five games that season when his running total would top the century mark.

Penn State completely dominated a hapless Army team at West Point, rolling up 45 unanswered points in a game that would have been even more one-sided had not Coach Paterno taken out the first team early in the third quarter to let his reserves finish out the afternoon. There was no attempt to roll up a ridiculous score: in the last 25 minutes of play Penn State didn't throw a single pass. Two of the Lion touchdowns on that gray afternoon were scored by John Cappelletti— both on short-yardage situations inside the Cadet five.

The sight of him crossing the goal line was becoming more and more familiar. Joey was counting up every touchdown. When cheers for the team began to be matched by cheers for *"Cappelletti,"* Joey seemed to take on new life. When the fans leaped to their feet in appreciation, after a score by John, Joey stood with them, fiercely proud of the secret he knew: it was his brother out there on the field.

The Penn State defense, the foot-soldiers so often ignored by offense-minded fans, contributed more than their share to the Lion victories that year. After blanking Army the defensive team went on to post its second consecutive shutout as Penn State stopped Syracuse 17-0. John Hufnagel scored all the points necessary when he sneaked over from the one in the second quarter. Reihner added a 42-yard field goal. And in the final quarter John capped his best running game of the season with a one-yard scoring plunge. On that Saturday the Lions amassed a total of 182 yards rushing. John had 162 yards, himself—nearly 90 percent of the team total.

Next day, Joey pored over the newspaper accounts of that game. Sports pages littered the living-room floor. The *Inquirer*'s story was headlined: "CAPPY LEADS LIONS ON RAMPAGE." Finally, Joey dropped the paper and dashed into the dining room where Anne was polishing the silverware.

"Mom, you want to toss the ball with me?"

"I'm busy, Joey. You can see that."

"Well, how'm I going to get to be any good, if I don't practice?"

"Go ahead. Practice. But let me do my work."

Joey dashed back to relive the game again by skimming through the newspapers. He knew all the Penn State starters and kept his own set of statistics. He knew what a fine year quarterback Hufnagel was having, but still he couldn't understand why his brother John didn't get more ink. The headline was there. Why didn't the story spend more time on individual plays? John was the one who deserved the cheers.

"Mom, watch," he said, trotting back to the dining-room. "You gotta help me with this." He posed like a cheerleader and shouted, "Gimme a C!"

Anne smiled and polished the spoon she was holding.

"Mom, are you going to help?"

"I'm sorry. C."

"You gotta yell!"

Anne shouted, "C!"

Delighted, Joey called out, "A!"

His one-woman cheering section responded with an "A!" Her hands were busy with the silver.

"P!"

"P!"

Joey leaped high in the air, shouting, "P!"

"I already said 'p.' "

"Come on, Mom. Now give me an E!"

"E!" Anne shouted.

"L!"

"L!"

"Another L!"

"And another L!"

"Now an E!"

"E!"

"T!"

"T!" She shouted, rolling her eyes. "Joey, if—"

"Now another T!"

Anne sagged. She laid down the spoon and looked

up at the ceiling. "Why couldn't I have married a man named Smith?"

"Awww, Mom!"

"Okay, another *T*!"

"*I*!"

"*I*!"

"What does it spell?" Joey poised himself for the final leap.

Together they shouted, *"Cap-Pel-Let-Ti!"*

Joey trotted over to stand beside his mother. "Okay, now let's do the other one."

"What other one?" Anne said, thinking *not again!*

"You know." Joey couldn't quite remember. He frowned in frustration. "Wait a minute." He dashed away to reappear with the newspaper, holding up the headline. "What the paper calls him."

"Oh," said Anne. "Cappy."

"Right!" Joey squinted at the headline, his finger pointing. "What's that dumb letter there?"

Anne leaned over to see what he meant. "That's a Y, Joey."

"Why can't I remember that one?"

A subtle cloud crossed Anne's face. It was at moments like this that she was forced to realize that the energetic boy beside her was still very sick. Most of the time she could overlook what she wasn't able to forget; but at a lapse in Joey's memory or a bit of clumsiness when he stumbled over his own feet and bumped into a chair or table, she was forced to remember. "Well," she said. "You keep working on it. You'll get it."

"Okay," Joey said. "Now—gimme a *C*!"

"Are we going to do all that again?"

"Awww, Mom!"

She put the spoon down and folded her arms. "Okay. *C*!"

Their practice wasn't wasted. Because the next weekend both those cheers—*"Cappelletti,"* and *"Cappy"*—resounded in Beaver Stadium and through the Penn State campus. It was one of John's best games of the season, and the cheerleaders down on the field kept as busy as the team. When the costumed mascot Lion began gamboling, or the blue and white cheerleaders leaped high into the air, their legs flashing in the sunlight, Joey nudged his mother and pointed, reminding her of the practice he'd led her through.

Banners in the student cheering section read "GO, CAPPY" and "CLOBBER THEM, CAPPY." The fans were shouting themselves hoarse. They had a lot to cheer about.

John scored in the first quarter from six yards out, and Vitiello's placekick put Penn State ahead 7-0. But Maryland soon tied the score. An exchange of field goals in the second quarter made the game a 10-10 tie when the teams went into the locker room. But in the second half Penn State blew the game wide open: John scored twice more, both on one-yard plunges, and quarterback John Hufnagel finished the day with 290 yards on 15 completions, a new school single-game record.

When the game had ended, the scoreboard read Penn State 46, Maryland 16.

The scene in the locker room was exuberant. Players shouted congratulations to each other, ignoring the bruises they'd feel on Sunday morning. At one end, Coach Paterno had been cornered by newsmen who were interviewing him. In front of his locker, John himself was trapped by a cameraman and a pair of reporters when his father entered the locker room, pushing through the knot of people clustered at the door and pulling Joey along by the hand. Once inside, Joey tugged his hand free.

"Hey, Joey! Whattaya say?" one of the players called.

"Good game, Tom," Joey answered.

Another player yelled, "You liked that one, did you?"

"Did I ever! You really robbed him on that one pass."

Eddie O'Neill, the 6'3", 225-pound linebacker,

shouted, "Joey! Hey, Joey, come here. I want to show you something."

"Hi, Eddie. Great game."

"I know. I was my usual incredible self." He rested a huge hand atop Joey's head, nearly covering it, and steered Joey off to the side and away from the worst of the noisy confusion. Dad watched them go, his characteristic restrained smile marking approval.

Of all the Penn State players, Eddie O'Neill was a favorite with Joey. Even bigger than John, and a terror on the field, O'Neill was a giant whose menacing glares made opposing running backs wish they'd found a hole that didn't open into O'Neill's area of responsibility. The threat of his slamming, bone-jarring tackles had persuaded some ball carriers that handling the ball wasn't the healthiest activity—when O'Neill was nearby. But all that ferocity was *on* the field. Off the field, and especially with Joey, he was jovial and gentle, in all his boasting the note of self-mockery.

"I want you to see this," O'Neill said. He pointed at John in front of his locker, flinching in the glare of flashbulbs. As fast as reporters fired questions, John answered them. But all the while he kept one hand inside his open locker, grasping a towel, in hopes they might take the hint and let him sneak off to the showers.

"What about it?" Joey asked.

"What *about* it? He's got reporters around him like flies around a hog-killing. Does anybody really want to read about a klutz like him?"

"He's no klutz," Joey said.

"I've seen *tractors* more graceful than he is!"

Joey returned the needling. "You're jealous because you're nothing but a linebacker."

O'Neill pantomimed terrible shock. His hands clasped at his throat in his best imitation of a silent film star choking to death. "Nothing but a *linebacker!* It's the highest calling in the athletic world. Grown men cry for the chance to play linebacker!"

"Come on," Joey said.

"Listen." O'Neill pushed Joey against a locker and knelt down to explain himself very carefully and logically. "How are you with numbers?"

"I don't know what you mean," Joey said, suspicious of the trap O'Neill was laying but willing to step into it.

"You know about fractions, right? Let me explain something. When somebody doesn't play this game very well, they make him a quarterback, okay?"

"O'Neill, I think you hurt your head out there today."

"No, listen. Then if he gets better at it, they promote him to halfback. You know—kind of middling good, like your brother." He waved away Joey's smiling objection before the boy could speak. "And after *half*back comes *full*back, y'see how it goes? Quarter, half, full? Okay, want to guess what comes after fullback?"

Joey laughed at what he could see coming next.

"You got it!" O'Neill said. "The highest calling in the athletic world, the only position for a real man! *Linebacker!*" He shouted a cheer and leaped high in the air.

Laughing harder than ever, Joey said, "A gorilla could play linebacker."

"Oh, now, that really hurt."

"Only, a gorilla would be too smart to want to."

"I'll kill him! I'll wipe him out!"

Two of O'Neill's teammates took hold of the linebacker's arms to hold him back.

"Get him out of here before I obliterate him," O'Neill called. He broke away from his teammates and scooped Joey up to hold him on his shoulder. He swung him around in a wide circle and set him down near John's locker, behind the reporters who were still asking questions.

"Go on," O'Neill said. "Break up that glory-hound's party. Introduce yourself."

Joey hung back, but the look on his face explained how much he really wanted to be inside the circle of

John's admirers. He looked up at O'Neill to say quietly, "Those guys aren't interested in me."

Always in spite of the welcome that O'Neill and the others regularly gave him, Joey had the sense of not quite belonging. The moment of glory he was watching belonged only to John. Joey was an outsider, and no matter how much the team members teased and played with him, he knew that the spotlight wasn't his. He was only a little boy, in the locker room temporarily, enjoying a moment in the shadow of his brother's achievement.

12

One football crowd resembles another. Their cheers are similar, and the colorful half-time shows are different only in minor ways. But after the game, no one wandering into the winning team's locker room could confuse the mood there with the gloom that blankets the losing team.

Hospitals are also similar. Tiled corridors echo to the sound of heels as visitors walk through them trying to be quiet out of concern for resting patients. Pages come over the intercom system: "Doctor Jamison wanted in Surgery." Or a phone call for some staff member identified only by a number, nurses and orderlies being paged—all hushed and muted and solemn. In a way Joey knew these sounds better than he knew the sounds of football Saturdays. He enjoyed them less.

In a corridor of Children's Hospital, Anne and Joey were emerging from an examining room, followed by a young resident, Doctor Klunick. To Anne, especially, the doctor looked very young, from his platform-soled shoes to the steel wool bush of his curly hair—young, but more than competent. His examination of Joey had been quick and thorough.

"Joey?" the doctor said. "Want to sit over there a few minutes? Your mother and I have to talk over a couple of things."

Joey headed for a chair beside the table covered with dog-eared copies of *Ranger Rick*, *Boy's Life*, and Walt Disney comics. His friend Mark already sat at the table, leaning forward and struggling to train a yo-yo that didn't seem interested in catching the knack of climbing the string back into his pudgy hand.

"Hi, Joey."

"Hello." Joey's answer was a monotone.

"Guess what. I'm going to get to be in the school band."

"That's great," Joey said. There was no excitement in his comment, only politeness. "What do you play?"

"I'm learning the cymbals." Mark laughed. "It's driving my big sister bananas. *Clang!*" He clapped his hands in imitation of the cymbals crashing. The yo-yo, tied to his finger and forgotten, swung out in a whistling arc and thumped to the tabletop, startling him.

Joey managed only a half-smile. He was inattentive and sat with his feet swinging.

"What's the matter with you?" Mark asked.

"I don't see why I have to come to this place when I'm not sick," Joey complained.

Mark looked at him, doubtful.

"I'm not! I'm not sick at all." In Joey's statement, his parents would have heard the boy's most fervent wish expressed. If will power alone had been enough, Joey would have healed himself long ago.

Inside the examining room Doctor Klunick pored over a pair of charts as he debated how to open the conversation.

Anne watched him anxiously, recognizing his hesitation. "Is anything wrong?" she asked.

He tapped a pencil against his teeth for a moment. "Well," he said, "since I've never examined Joey before . . ." His voice faded, evasion apparent in the way he looked from one corner of the room to the other and avoided her eyes. It was his third parent conference of the day; neither of the other two had been easy.

"What is it?"

"To be frank with you, I'm a little concerned about some of his reflexes. You see, in a neurological work-up—"

Anne interrupted. "The bilateral Babinski wasn't negative, was it?" Concern in her very posture, she leaned closer to the doctor.

Startled, Doctor Klunick said, "No, it wasn't, but—"

"Wouldn't reflex changes be fairly normal for someone who'd been in a coma that long?"

"He was in a coma?" The doctor leaned back in his chair.

Anne took a deep breath and weighed her words as carefully as the doctor had weighed his a moment earlier. "Joey's case history is so long, I'm not surprised you didn't get to read it all. The other doctors told me the Biserpedine might affect him for quite a while."

Doctor Klunick flipped through the thick folder in his hands—Joey's records—skimming the pages. "When . . . When did he have Biserpedine?"

From her purse Anne drew out a small but thick loose-leaf notebook. She flipped through it with a quick, practiced hand until her moving index finger found the entry she wanted. "His last dose was on February eighth."

"What is that you've got there?"

"This?" Anne held up the notebook. "Oh, it's just that so many doctors have worked on Joey over the years, I thought I ought to take notes and keep track of things, in case they had any questions."

"What sort of information do you keep?"

Anne said simply, "Everything."

After a pause, Doctor Klunick asked, "*Every*thing?"

"Yes." Anne thumbed through the notebook to remind herself. The doctor knew even better than she the particular drugs whose names she'd jotted down —some administered, some only discussed, a few she had read about and wanted defined in conversation: Prednisone, Methetrexate, Mercaptopurine, Cytosine arabinoside, Thioguanine, Asparaginase. He didn't need details on tests administered to measure and evaluate Joey's blood levels of white cells, platelets, hemoglobin. She summarized for him: "Joey's temperature, every time it was taken. All the medication, the results of all his tests and when they were given to him, his weight gains . . . and losses." She looked up from the handwritten pages. "Is there something new that's wrong?"

"No." He rose to pace for a moment. "No, I'm sure the coma explains what I noticed."

Anne was uneasy. "I'm not trying to make you embarrassed, Doctor."

"I'm not, though I probably should be." He stopped and turned to face her with a thoughtful look. He'd never met anyone who'd kept such detailed records; in fact he doubted that the folder he'd been glancing through could match the detail Mrs. Cappelletti had recited. "That's a remarkable thing for you to have done," he said.

Anne was embarrassed. She had never considered it remarkable before, only common sense. "Not really," she said. "I thought someone ought to keep track."

"And you went to—"

"My husband helped," Anne interrupted. "We all did."

"That's not what I mean. What I meant was . . ." He smiled. "I think you understand."

"It seemed like a sensible thing to do," she said. She tucked the notebook back into her purse and rose. "Then, there isn't anything new wrong with Joey?"

"Nothing new." Doctor Klunick shook Anne's hand and watched her leave the room, a lighter spring in her step. The satisfaction she'd taken from his answer buoyed him. He followed her into the corridor in time to see her take Joey's hand and start for the elevator. The simple sight of them let him look forward to his next scheduled examination with anticipation he hadn't felt all day.

13

Seven-and-one after the Maryland game, the Penn State team was in high gear and rolling. North Carolina State brought a record of 6-2-1 into Beaver Stadium, riding the crest of a five-game winning streak. Penn State blew them out. The first score of the day—it was getting to be a habit—was John's, but in this case different from most of his scores that season. Rather than blasting in from the one or two, he caught a 33-yard pass for the touchdown to start the scoring. At halftime the Lions led 23-0 and had built their lead to 30-8 early in the fourth quarter. With the outcome no longer in doubt, in went the reserves. N.C. State salvaged some pride by putting fourteen more points on the board late in a game that ended with the Nittany Lions on top 37-22.

John opened the scoring at Boston College's Alumni Stadium the next Saturday, pounding over from the one in the first quarter. A seesaw battle decided finally by Penn State's superior fire power, the game saw brilliant plays by both teams. The score mounted and mounted, but B.C. couldn't match the Lion output and ended the day on the short end of a 45-26 score. Nine wins, one loss, and the Penn State season had a single game to go.

It was another romp, 49–27 over Pittsburgh, a game even more one-sided than the score indicated. In the third quarter, with the Lions up 42–0, Paterno cleared his bench. Cappelletti, Hufnagel, and other starters on offense and defense as well, spent the rest of the game cheering the reserves. Pitt was outmanned by the Penn State regulars but enough superior to third- and fourth-stringers to score four touchdowns in the final quarter and make the newspaper accounts seem like descriptions of a real contest.

The '72 season ended with the Lions in proud possession of a record of 10 wins, one loss. Bowl invitations were being sent out, and Christmas was near.

Christmas came twice to the Cappelletti home that year. One celebration was held early because Penn State was scheduled to play in the Sugar Bowl in New Orleans and John wouldn't be home with the family on December 25. When the invitation had come through and the Sugar Bowl opponents were decided, Joey had been unhappy . . . and pleased, at the same time: he was looking forward to seeing John play before millions of TV viewers, but he was disappointed that John wouldn't be home with him to celebrate Christmas.

And then he was pleased to learn of the double Christmas the family would have . . . but disappointed that he couldn't accompany his parents to New Orleans to see the game firsthand. It was a confusing time for Joey. His moods changed from moment to moment and he was never quite certain whether to enjoy the extra pleasures he had on hand or lament those he would miss later on. Being the boy he was, he finally settled for the happier view . . . most of the time.

On the evening of their first Christmas celebration, torn wrapping paper and tangled ribbon littered the living-room floor. A decorated Norway pine stood in the corner, a star atop it reflecting the colored lights that surrounded the tree and flashed through the shimmering coat of tinsel hanging like so many icicles from the blue-green branches. In the bay window stood the crèche scene that Anne was so proud of: carved figures some fifteen inches high—Mary and Joseph and the shepherds kneeling beside the manger under a faint blue light, and visible to passersby outside.

The women—Anne, Jean, and Joyce—lingered over coffee while John and Dad stowed small handtools in a toolkit Dad had received. Joey, on his way to bed, came downstairs from his bedroom wearing pajamas. "Good night!" he called.

Three voices from the dining room echoed, "Good night!"

"Night, Hoss," John said.

Joey walked over to him. "Are you going to be gone when I get up?"

"Yeah, I'll be rolling out pretty early. You stay in bed. Don't worry about me."

"I don't see why you have to leave tomorrow, when the game isn't till New Year's."

"Coach wants us to get used to the climate in New Orleans," John told him.

"I'd like to get used to that," Dad said.

"You will," Anne called. "Don't be impatient."

Joey said, "I'm glad we could have Christmas before you left."

"I'll bet you are. That way you get to have two of them." John poked a stiff finger at Joey's ribs.

But Joey danced out of reach. "You're going to clobber Oklahoma."

"Hear that, Dad?"

John Sr. nodded.

"Now you and Mom don't even have to come down and see the game. It's all settled."

Joey walked over to give John a hug. "Well, I *hope* you do, anyway."

"Stay well, now," John said.

"I will." Joey waved to everyone. "Good night," he said again, and walked up the steps.

John watched him go, marveling at his brother's vitality. He turned and spoke to his father. "I wish Joey could make the trip with you."

"He understands why he can't."

"Well, I wouldn't mind if you think you ought to stay here with him. I can always—"

Dad thumped John on the arm. "John, you're important to us, too. Now I don't want to hear any more about it. We're going to be there, and Joey will be fine."

That was decided. John nodded and walked away. His father settled back into a chair and reached over to turn on the radio to Christmas carols, which played softly in the quiet room.

Just beyond the kitchen was a den that John Sr. had added to the house, its paneled walls covered with plaques. Four shelves were laden with trophies that Marty and John and Michael had won in high school and summer-league athletics. All three sons, at different schools, had been chosen most valuable player of the year in one sport or another. For John, at Monsignor Bonner High School, it had been all sports. Baseball and football trophies bore Michael's name: at Malvern Prep he'd been an all-League fullback. And Martin had starred in the same sports at St. Joseph's Prep. There were literally scores of trophies and awards in the room—a matter of real pride to John Sr., who had never played interscholastic sports himself. But the room was not a display case. Like Dad himself it was unobtrusive and solid rather than showy. The trophies sat back against the wall on their shelves, and anyone entering the room for the first time was struck not by them but by the battered leather couch along one wall —a pair of reading lamps bracketing it—and the sense of quiet comfort the room conveyed.

Across the room from the couch was a console TV set, and in front of the couch at the moment John entered the room was a small folding table. Mike and Marty faced each other across the table in combat— playing gin rummy.

"Mike?" John asked, "d'you think I could take your beige sweater with me?"

Michael looked up. "Just be sure you don't get any lipstick on it." He winked at Marty.

"Where would I get lipstick? Paterno's going to keep us in prison till the game."

"Mike? Pay attention?" Marty had drawn and was preparing to discard. "I don't want you to miss this." He fanned his cards and laid them on the tabletop. "Name-of-the-game, 'gin.' "

Michael slumped back on the couch. "See what happens when I don't concentrate? You did it to me again."

"Older and wiser is the rule." Marty looked up. "Want to play, John?"

"I don't think so." John seemed distracted.

Noticing his vacant stare, Marty asked, "What's the matter with you tonight?"

"Oh, it bothers me. That's all."

"What does?" Marty picked up the cards and began to shuffle them.

"I don't know why I'm so lucky, and it bothers me."

Michael twisted around on the couch to sit upright. "What are you so lucky *at?*"

Leaning against the doorjamb with his arms folded, John explained. "I'm doing something I really love. Playing football. And because I'm lucky enough to be good at it, all these terrific things happen to me. Like this trip, for instance."

Michael grinned at Marty. "That's right. The luck of that guy would amaze you. Did he ever tell you about the lottery?"

"What lottery?"

The grin was wider now, as Michael explained. "Paterno didn't have any idea who he was going to use at tailback this year, so he drew a number out of a hat, and it turned out to be twenty-two. That's the only reason John's been starting this season. Just dumb luck."

"I'm serious, Mike." John was quiet and solemn.

His brothers knew him well enough to understand when the time for kidding had passed.

"Sorry, John," Michael said.

"You're talking about Joey," Martin said. It wasn't a question. John's voice had taken on a special quality that Marty recognized.

"Yeah, I guess I am. But what kind of sense does it make for Joey to have it so rough, and me to have it so easy?"

The question hung in the room, unanswered—and unanswerable.

But John didn't have it easy in New Orleans. Always strong as a granite building, never sick or injured, John was knocked flat on his back by a virus. What opposing teams hadn't been able to accomplish all year, an invisible organism did: it crippled the Penn State offense. John spent December 31 in bed in his hotel room.

Anne and Dad, who had come all the way to New Orleans to watch John play in the Sugar Bowl, were with him, Anne feeding him juices and aspirin, taking his temperature, while Dad sat beside John to watch a telecast of the game John couldn't play in.

If John was knocked flat that New Year's Eve, so was Penn State. The final score was Oklahoma 14, Penn State 0. But even in his misery, he knew that no matter how rotten he felt at that moment, *his* illness would pass. A day or two, he'd be as healthy and strong as ever.

For Joey, it was different . . .

SPRING 1973

14

Throughout the next spring term, John kept busy with his studies. For several months running he had the rare opportunity to devote all his energies to the classroom and library. A Law Enforcement major at Penn State, he worked hard at his courses and was even able to combine a semester-long project with two trips back to Upper Darby—where he spoke with local police officers and studied methods of law enforcement at the borough level.

He spent his spring vacation as well as those two weekends together with Joey. Football was nearly forgotten. The Philadelphia *Bulletin* and *Inquirer* featured items about the Phillies' training camp in Florida. The team, sportswriters said, looked likely to come back from a weak showing the year before. But in spring training every team's a possible champion—it's the annual optimism that follows the rising thermometer up out of winter's depression.

The arrival of spring brought football practice with it; after April 1, John had two full-time occupations again—student and running back—and there were no more visits home.

Spring showed itself at the Cappelletti home in its usual bright colors: the forsythia was a sprawling yellow waterfall; dogwood trees were budding, azaleas blossomed and crocuses lined the sidewalk with white, yellow and lavender. All these signs pointed toward the new excitement Joey had been waiting for: the start of the baseball season was only a few warm days ahead.

While the Phillies soaked out winter's kinks in the Florida sun, Philadelphia boys were going through their own spring training. In basements, back yards and muddy lots, they gathered to show off brand-new baseballs which, in mere weeks, would be crisscrossed with black friction tape to replace the battered covers.

Joey sat on the front porch, rubbing neat's-foot oil into the palm of Michael's old glove and watching the sky for good-news sunshine.

His father had agreed to coach the Cardinals in the Pee Wee League—very much like Little League but less self-consciously an imitation of the majors: a few rules differed from the Williamsport code. One of those rules would work to Joey's benefit: each boy on the team had to play in every game.

Dad had taken on the task of coaching, just as he'd done earlier when Marty and then John and finally Michael were Pee Wee League members. He wanted to be on hand to watch his sons and—in this case—to make certain that Joey wasn't pressured by a coach and teammates unaware of Joey's physical problems. It wasn't a matter of protecting Joey so much as giving the boy the chance to work as hard as possible within the limits of his abilities. His father knew those limits, and he also knew Joey's determination.

Observatory Hill Park where they practiced was a short drive from home. Two evenings a week Joey and his father loaded bats, balls, catcher's equipment, bases and a pitcher's rubber in the trunk of the car and drove to the field in time to set up the diamond before the other Cardinals got there. Marty met them. He was assistant coach on the team; and together Dad and Marty worked the nine-, ten-, and eleven-year-old boys through their paces, teaching them the game as well as helping them enjoy the practice sessions.

Joey still suffered problems with coordination, and his difficulty with peripheral vision made him less than a threat at the plate: the slightest lapse in concentration and he lost sight of the pitch while he swung at it. That can happen to any batter who lets his head move during his swing, but Joey's problem was compounded by an inability to catch sight of the ball until it had nearly reached him. Difficulties or not, no one worked harder or had more dedicated coaching.

On most Tuesday and Thursday evenings at practice sessions, a few parents stopped by to lounge on the new green grass behind the backstop or sit on folding lawn chairs they brought with them. A small section of bleachers stood behind home plate, but the parents tended to string out along the foul lines beyond third and first to watch their sons. Marty and Dad split coaching duties. While Marty took a group of outfielders over to one corner of the block-square field and hit fungoes to them, his father worked with the rest of the team at the plate. One evening he pitched for over an hour, all the boys taking their turns with the bat. He made no special concession to Joey; for him, as for all the Cardinals, he threw the ball straight and easy, down the middle, giving them all the opportunity to take their swings with the small aluminum bat. Part of what he wanted was to build their confidence.

But Joey never once hit so much as a foul ball. His coordination was so poor that his swing was usually far too late, even when he didn't lose sight of the ball, but he never complained. He took his five cuts and a bunt, then walked to the end of the queue to wait his next turn. If Dad occasionally glanced at Joey, working his way to the head of the line and one more siege of disappointment, he said nothing to the boy that he didn't also tell the others.

"Remember now," he told them. "Back elbow up, stride with the pitch, watch the ball all the way to the bat." He said the same thing to all of them, showing Joey no favoritism while the other boys were there.

But after practice had ended and the other Cardinals dashed off whooping in excitement to their parents' cars, Marty caught, Dad pitched, and Joey swung and swung and tried his best to follow Marty's low-voiced batting hints. He didn't seem discouraged though he had every reason to be. The extra practice wasn't helping at all.

Some Saturday mornings the team met at Observatory Hill Park, occasionally for practice games but more often to drill. Marty hit grounders to the infielders who practiced their throws across the miniature

diamond to first base. They chucked the ball around
in conscious imitation of the major-leaguers they had
seen on television. So many of them had the stance
down to perfection, the graceful moves, they seemed
more like miniature adults than children. The Cardinal
shortstop in particular looked like the Phillies' own
Bobby Wine, or even more the new Phillies rookie,
Larry Bowa: fast, active, aggressive, noisy, he could
dart quickly to his right, backhand the ball, wheel in
one fluid motion . . . and then the illusion faded. He
became a child again and threw the ball to first base
on two bounces. Dad and Marty fought back their
smiles and kept the boys practicing.

On one of those Saturdays, Anne, Jean and Joyce
came to watch Joey practice. They sat in the bleachers
just behind home plate.

Jean especially was concerned at the way batting
practice went for Joey. "No wonder he can't hit the
ball," she said. "He can't see it coming."

Anne knew that wasn't important. "He can try," she
said. "Nobody's asking more than that."

The three women called encouragement to Joey. He
told his teammates that it embarrassed him to have
those "girls" watching and commenting on "boy's
stuff," but he secretly enjoyed their attention.

Many of the boys had trouble hitting the ball; Joey
wasn't alone in that. But when his turn came to take
the field, shagging fly balls that Marty hit to him, his
difficulty stood out in sharper relief. He couldn't judge
the flight of the ball and it was as likely to land six or
eight feet from him as it was to touch his glove.

"Joey," his father called. "It's landing at your feet.
Only a couple of steps in, get under it."

All determination, Joey tugged his cap lower, hitched
up his belt, and said, "Right."

Marty hit another pop-up and Joey ran to get under
it, but the ball sailed over his head. He muttered angrily and trotted back to retrieve it.

Watching all this, Jean asked, "Mom? How's he going to compete with the other boys?"

"He'll do his best."

Joyce nodded. "Dad won't put him in the lineup if he doesn't think he'll do okay."

"Every boy has to play every game," Anne told her. "Those are league rules."

"Terrific!" Jean said.

"It's all right. Dad said he'd probably use him in right field, in the last inning."

"It's a good idea," Joyce said. "He'll be playing without having too many chances to look silly."

Jean was still doubtful. "Mom, he could be humiliated even then. Can't you talk him out of it?"

"Did I ever try to talk you out of anything? Joey wants to try, and he's going to get his chance."

Unconvinced, Jean looked out at the field where Joey was still making futile attempts to catch the ball. Marty dropped the fungo bat and by hand tossed a soft, easy fly to Joey. Joey got his glove on it but again dropped it. He clenched his teeth till the muscles in his jaw stood out but he said nothing. He walked after it, snatched it up angrily and threw it awkwardly back to his brother. Some inner determination kept driving him.

Joey's difficulties could be laid partly to inexperience, partly to the lingering effect of his long coma. John, who had begun spring football practice at University Park, had problems too, of another sort. His were physical. As the starting running back in Paterno's varied offense—principally Winged-T and Power-I— he'd already taken a beating. He knew the system well enough that learning his individual assignments gave him no trouble. But it was another matter to carry the ball as often as he did against one of the finest defensive units in the country: his own team, Penn State. Practice sessions put a big, hungry, mobile line across the ball from John.

To come sprinting along the line looking for an opening was almost instinctive for John. He'd take a quick pitch and head right for the corner to make his turn, but if a gap appeared inside the end he cut back quickly to his left. More often than not, filling that fast-closing hole in the defensive line was 6'3", 225-pound Eddie O'Neill. And the thud of their collisions was enough to give bruises to the sympathetic, wincing spectators.

After practice, John spent many painful minutes on the rubdown table or sitting in a whirlpool bath to soak out bruises and loosen knotted muscles. On one liniment-scented afternoon he was sitting in the whirlpool with his arms hooked over the stainless-steel rim of the tank, his legs stretched out in front of him and his eyes closed, when Eddie O'Neill walked in.

"Cappy, wake up."

John opened one eye slowly. "I'm awake."

"Uh-huh. You awake enough to open your mail? You had a couple things back at the FIJI house." Eddie stopped beside the whirlpool and held out a letter to John.

"Hand me a towel?"

"Can I dry your hands for you?" Eddie snatched a towel off the pile on the floor beside him. "Would you like a manicure while I'm here?"

"Okay, okay. Just give me the letter."

"If you didn't loaf away every afternoon in your little dunk-tub, you could fetch your own mail."

"Uh-huh," John said. "And if you didn't thump me with that cast-iron skull of yours, I wouldn't need this tub. The mail?"

Eddie laughed and handed John the envelope. He pulled a stool up next to the whirlpool and sat down to open his own mail.

They read in silence until John began to chuckle softly.

"You want to swap?" Eddie asked. "Mine's never as hilarious as yours."

John held up a clipping. "Joey sent me an article he wrote for his school paper."

"About . . . ?"

"Uh . . . me."

Eddie nodded. "I had to ask."

"Be quiet a minute, I'll tell you what it says. Get this." John read from the clipping. " 'John's gentle as a summer breeze on a summer night, but put a football in his hand and he's dynamite.' "

"Better than Muhammad Ali," Eddie said. He watched John read a few more lines in silence before he said, "How's he doing?"

"Okay, I guess." It had been so long since John had seen Joey that he frowned at Eddie's innocent question. Then he brightened and returned to the letter in his hand. "As far as baseball's concerned, he tells me he's burning up the league. No, listen. I'll read you what he really says. 'I think there's a good chance I'll be a superstar just like' . . ." His voice faded and he stopped reading with a shrug.

"Well? Just like *what?*"

"Skip it," John said, and turned away.

O'Neill reached out to snatch the letter from John's hand.

"Hey! Let me have that."

"No, no, *no!* You're keeping secrets," O'Neill said. "I'll read it for myself." He skimmed down the page until he found the interrupted passage. "Here it is. He says, 'I think there's a good chance I'll be a superstar just like . . . *you.*' Oh, wow!" O'Neill's smirk was lightly mocking. "Two superstars in one family, how 'bout that?"

John scooped a handful of water from the whirlpool and threw it at O'Neill. Then he said, "At least we're both getting to play."

O'Neill looked at him for a moment, his recollections of Joey vivid and sharp in memory, and said, "It's a point." He handed the letter back.

Joey could be forgiven some exaggeration in his letters to John. His lack of success on the diamond embarrassed him, made him angry and frustrated, and was exactly the sort of failure he couldn't describe to John.

In mid-May the Cardinals were in a crucial game against the Giants, the team they shared first place with in the league standings. It was the seventh, final inning of the game, two outs, bases loaded—one of those do-or-die situations that Hollywood likes to offer on the screen. But Hollywood or not, situations like that do arise—and Joey was at the plate.

He was absolutely terrified. There was almost no place in the world he wouldn't rather have been at that moment, but the lineup was fixed and there was nothing to be done, no magic solution or mysterious pinch-hitter to step out of the dugout and into the spotlight in Joey's stead.

On the bench along first base the other Cardinals shouted encouragement to him. Around the infield the Giants talked it up to bolster the pitcher's courage. Excited, soprano chattering filled the air, and behind the bench at first the Cardinals' seven-year-old bat-boy, younger brother of the team pitcher, was standing on a stepladder before the scoreboard with numbered cards in his hands, ready to hang one of them on the scoreboard. Under the name "CARDINALS" the seventh inning was empty, and the boy held placards with 1 and 2 on them—the first would show a tie game, the second a Cardinal win. He teetered atop the stepladder, his eyes round in anticipation, shouting along with everyone else.

The pitcher checked the runners on base, set, delivered. Joey's swing missed the ball by at least a foot. Spectators shouted to their sons, or friends. On the next pitch, Joey swung with all his might—before the ball reached the plate. It landed with a smack in the catcher's mitt.

The catcher lobbed the ball back to the pitcher, yelling, "We got him! This guy's easy. Fire it in here, babe!"

The pitcher surveyed the infield; Cardinal runners held their bases but leaned toward the right, hands on right knee, ready to take off as soon as the ball reached the plate.

Joey muttered to himself, "Eye on the ball. Meet it, don't kill it, just try to meet it." It was the batter's litany, a chant of self-encouragement that sounded like an incantation.

The Giant pitcher leaned forward, gloved hand resting on his left knee, looked down at his catcher, went into the windup, and fired. Joey's swing missed by nearly two feet.

The Giant infielders tossed their gloves in the air with elation and whooped over their triumph while the base runners turned to trudge dejectedly toward the bench. Joey fought to keep the tears from coming. He dropped the bat at the plate and walked away.

Coming down from his coaching box at third base, Dad Cappelletti picked up the bat and crossed the diamond to load equipment in his car.

When Joey and his father got home and entered the kitchen, Anne was preparing supper. "Well? How'd it go?" she asked.

Joey muttered something unintelligible and slammed his glove into the corner. He opened the refrigerator door.

"Not one of our better days," Dad said.

"How did you do, Joey?"

Dad shook his head quickly, asking her not to press the question.

Instantly taking the cue, Anne said, "Well, there'll be another game next week, and—"

"Strawberry, nothing but strawberry!" Joey complained. "Why isn't there ever any grape in this stupid refrigerator?"

"Joey, watch your tongue now," Anne said.

Joey only got louder. "I tell you a thousand times that I *hate* strawberry and you don't pay any attention to me!"

Dad crossed to him. "All right, Joey. That's enough."

Now the boy was yelling. "Nobody ever pays any attention to me! *Nobody!*"

Calmly Dad seized Joey's arm, turned him around and with his other hand swatted him in the seat of the pants. Joey glared angrily at his father before the angry expression dissolved in tears. Then Dad pulled Joey into a loose embrace.

Anxiously, Anne said, "Did you hurt him, John?" There was more than a touch of accusation in her voice.

With a smile, Dad said, "My handprint will be on his bottom for a year, at least."

Joey pulled away from his father's shirtfront, wiping his eyes on his sleeve. "That's not why I'm crying, 'cause Dad spanked me."

"I know, son," his father said comfortingly. "I know."

"Then what's the matter?" Anne said. "The game? It's only a game, Joey."

"You know what's going to happen?" he said. "John's going to come home and he's going to come to the game and he's going to think I'm the dumbest klutz he ever saw!"

"Come on, now. Johnny won't think that." Anne tried to cheer him up.

"Yes he will, Mom." He stared at the floor, thinking. "I'm going to quit the team."

Before Anne could voice any protest, Dad waved her off with a gesture. "Okay," he said to Joey. "That's up to you. Of course, John will want to know why you quit."

"I'll tell him I got tired of practicing."

Dad reached into the refrigerator and took out two soft drinks. He stood with his head cocked, considering Joey's comment. "Mmmm, not too good."

"Why not?"

"I'm sure John gets tired of practicing. And he's been doing it a lot longer than you have. How's that going to sound to him?" Dad opened one of the bottles and handed it to Joey. He tossed the screwtop cap casually in one hand.

By now, his tears gone, Joey was honestly asking advice. "What should I do then?" he said.

"I wonder what John would do?" Dad seemed fascinated by the bottlecap he flipped. He spoke casually, as if he had no interest in Joey's answers.

"I don't know," said Joey.

"Do you think he'd quit?" Dad opened his bottle and took a drink from it, after tucking the bottlecaps into his shirt pocket.

"John? No, but he's *good!*"

"Can you imagine how dumb he felt the time he fumbled on the two-yard line?"

Joey nodded. "Yeah."

Watching and listening through the entire exchange, Anne saw the outcome developing.

"I don't think I've ever known John to quit," Dad said. "Of course, that doesn't mean *you* can't."

Deep in thought, Joey stared at the bottle he held in his hand without even seeing it. When he finally spoke he said, "I don't really want to."

"Then don't," his father said casually. He took another drink from his bottle and reached over to ruffle Joey's hair, peering over his head at Anne, who was smiling broadly now. He rolled his eyes for her benefit, embarrassed at the transparency of his ploy in persuading Joey to stick with the team.

But transparent to Anne or not, the conversation had made good sense to Joey. His jaw was set in fresh determination: there'd be no chance of his giving up now. He couldn't picture John as a quitter.

15

For the Cardinals the season was successful, more successful than it was for Joey personally. League organizers had wisely split the schedule into two halves —each half to end with a "champion" atop the standings—creating two seasons in one. And although the Cards lost the first half of the split season to the Giants because of their one-run loss, when the second half ended in mid-June they were in first place.

And that meant a playoff. In some seasons, during Michael's years in Pee Wee League for instance, the same team had won both halves and could spend the rest of the summer boasting about their invincibility; but in the summer of '73 the question of baseball supremacy among nine- and ten-year-olds in

the Highland Park-Kirklyn Athletic Association remained unsettled. It wasn't an issue to rank with tear-
ing down the Berlin Wall . . . except to the boys
involved.

The playoff game was set for a Saturday afternoon.
With the term at Penn State over, John was home and
able to attend the game, a possibility he'd looked forward to with every one of Joey's letters since April.
That morning he caught Joey sitting glumly on the
front steps, staring at the street out front.

"Feeling down, Joey?"

"What? Oh, no. I'm okay."

"Want to throw a couple, loosen up your arm for
the game?"

"Not now, John. Thanks. Maybe I'll go inside."

John sat and watched his brother walk away, bewildered at the mood of depression he recognized in
Joey. He decided it must be only tension and concern
about the game that afternoon.

And he was right, in a way. But if he'd known how
the season had gone for Joey—not so much as hitting
a foul ball at the plate, errors and missed plays in
right field—he would have understood his mood better. Today the brother whose football victories Joey
had cheered was on hand to watch his failure. That
was the boy's conviction: the game would prove his
worthlessness to John. John wouldn't be proud of him.

Nevertheless Joey said nothing about his fears, and
after lunch the family piled into two cars—Joey to
ride with Joyce and Marty—and drove to the playground at St. Laurence Elementary School for the
game.

Accustomed to 50,000 cheering fans and more in
the stadiums he played in, John might not have seen
the fifty people on hand for that game as a "crowd."
To Joey, the whole world was present, and every single
one of them was staring at him, alone. In fact it was a
lighthearted group of parents, some picnicking along
the foul-lines, others exchanging greetings in the
bleachers behind home plate, where the Cappelletti
family sat. Marty and his father were busy coaching

their team, but the rest of the family had settled onto the wooden benches, relaxing. Anne talked to a neighbor, Jean and Joyce discussed a movie they had seen the preceding week, and Michael tilted his head back, eyes closed, to let the warm sun lull him into a lethargy just this side of sleep. All the tension was out on the diamond.

The Giants jumped out to a quick lead and at the end of three innings were ahead 4–0, thanks to a pitcher who threw with the authority of someone in his teens. But league rules forbade any pitcher to work more than three innings, and the Giants' starter was their best. When both teams changed pitchers to begin the fourth inning, the Cards began chipping away at the Giants' lead.

At the end of six the score was 4–3, Giants. Once more substitutions were made: every boy in uniform had to play, and for a few of them that had meant a single inning in each game during the season. The championship game was no different. Joey trotted out to right field.

"Now we'll get 'em!" John shouted, trying unsuccessfully to catch Joey's eye.

The Cardinal defense held in the top of the seventh, and the boys came trooping in for their last turn at bat, only one run down with a chance to tie, or possibly even to win, the game. By now the tension on the field had reached the stands, and even those parents who earlier had kept only half their attention on the game sat leaning forward, waiting.

"Hang in there, Cards!" Michael called.

"Three outs and you got 'em!" countered one of the Giant boosters.

The Cards lead-off hitter in the seventh walked and the Cardinal bench came to life. Boys shouted and waved their caps and threw catcalls at the nervous Giant pitcher, until Dad Cappelletti motioned for them to keep it down a little. The Giant infield tried to drown out those catcalls with their own shrill encouragement to their pitcher; except for their high-pitched voices, they might have been major-leaguers seen through the wrong end of a telescope. They moved well around the bases, crouched hands-on-knees in readiness, all in imitation of the National League stars they'd watched play at Philadelphia's Veterans Stadium.

The pitcher dug in and struck out the next batter. The one to follow popped up and the Giants first-baseman took the lazy, twisting foul right in front of the Cards bench, squeezing the ball in spite of the hoots and cries of Cardinal players trying to startle him into an error. Two down, a runner on first, and the Giant infield was louder than ever—victory for them a single out away.

"C'mon, Kevin!" Marty shouted from the first-base coaching box. "Give it a ride!"

"Take him downtown!" Michael shouted from the bleachers behind home plate, reaching over to pound on John's arm.

The Cards shortstop walked to the plate while his teammates on the bench shouted encouragement, a note of desperation in their voices. Two outs, and Kevin represented their last chance.

"No pitcher, no pitcher!" one of the boys said.

"You can hit this guy!" shouted another.

Sitting on one end of the bench, Joey muttered, "Strike out, Kevin. Or pop up."

He said it quietly, but not so quietly that the pitcher seated next to him hadn't heard. The boy whirled around in amazement. "Joey! We're only a run behind! We can beat these guys!"

Joey said, "Yeah. But if Kevin gets a hit, I'll have to bat."

"Oh yeah . . . I forgot." The pitcher nodded and fell silent.

On the first pitch Kevin slammed a clean single over the second baseman's head into right field. The runner on first took off and rounded second, hesitated a moment, then kept going when he saw the right-fielder momentarily bobble the ball. The long throw to third base was too late, the base runner was safe, and on the throw Kevin went into second standing up.

The cheering from the stands was louder now, and the Cardinal bench emptied as the boys screamed frantically. They yelled at the base runners, at one another, at nothing, just for the excuse to yell. All of them but Joey. His father, coaching at third base, looked toward the bench and waved encouragement. Joey shrugged nervously and walked over to choose a bat and a plastic batting helmet.

John saw him coming to the plate. "Hey, Joey! Hit one out!"

"That's right, Joey," Jean said. "Do what you can."

John looked at her strangely—what kind of encouragement was that? But then he hadn't watched Joey in practice, as the rest of the family had.

Joey heard his brother's voice and managed a small smile of acknowledgement, though he felt anything but happy. He took his place in the batter's box. The aluminum bat was slippery to his sweating palms so he gripped it tighter and clenched his teeth till his jaw ached.

The Giant pitcher fired, and as always Joey's roundhouse swing missed the ball by several inches.

"You can do it, now!"

"Bring me in, Joey!" Kevin stood on second, his left foot holding the bag and his right stretched toward third as far as he could reach without leading off illegally.

Marty clapped and paced in the first-base coach's box. "Be tough, Joey! Make him pitch to you!"

The pitcher wound, and threw, and this time the ball hit a good two feet in front of the plate, skidding in the dirt. Joey started his swing but held back in time.

"Ball one."

It was a moral victory, at least. Joey hadn't missed the pitch, and he tried to find comfort in that.

"At-a-way, Hoss, way to look!" John shouted again. Anne called, "Come on, Joey!"

Jean and Michael joined in the cheering. At the plate Joey wore a determined frown. The pitcher looked so huge to him, the ball so tiny—a mere pellet that traveled at supersonic speed.

The Giant catcher trotted halfway to the mound, called something to the pitcher and tossed the ball to him underhand. Spectators leaned forward on the wooden benches. The coaches prowled in their coaching boxes—Marty with his cap tugged low to keep the sun out of his eyes and Dad pacing more slowly, hands on hips—while both teams were on their feet now behind the cyclone fence of the backstop, calling out whatever encouragement they could think of. Tension mounted as the pitcher looked in. Of everyone there that day, John was easily the most relaxed. He clapped and whistled as the pitcher toed the rubber.

Joey would rather have been standing in front of a firing squad, but when the pitcher went into his wind-up and threw the ball, Joey closed his eyes tightly and swung with all his strength.

There was a sharp *crack* and Joey opened his eyes in total astonishment.

The ball kicked off the pitcher's mound toward second base where the shortstop lunged for it but missed, sprawling on the ground as the ball went through into left-center field. Both baserunners raced around to score the tying and then the winning runs, the throw came into the plate too late, and Joey crossed first base safely with his only hit of the season. He hadn't gone two feet beyond the bag when Marty grabbed him in his arms and hoisted him into the air. All the other Cardinal players scrambled to surround them, cheering and shouting, Dad Cappelletti running across the diamond to join the excitement. In the bleachers, parents leaped up shouting in delight or sat in stunned silence. Bobby Thompson's 1951 homer at the Polo Grounds couldn't have spawned more delirium.

The Giants, disconsolate, trudged off the field, a few of them crying in frustration till their coach gathered them in a milling circle to commiserate with them.

In the bleachers, Anne, Jean, Michael, Joyce, John were all on their feet cheering at the top of their voices. John pounded Michael on the back excitedly until Michael escaped the thudding barage of fists.

Joey's teammates mobbed him. Jostled and pushed, his cap snatched off, he was dazed but delighted. And when he looked up to see his brother John leading the family onto the field in the midst of the wonderful bedlam, Joey yelled, "You think you're the only star in this family, Yo-yo?"

John laughed uproariously and stood aside to watch the hero of the hour sweep past him on his teammates' shoulders.

16

That summer everyone in the family was busy. Michael had a job as a playground aide. His father was putting in a lot of overtime on the job because his construction crew had fallen behind schedule; they were at work on a hotel and parking-garage complex planned to accommodate some of the crowds expected in Philadelphia for the upcoming Bicentennial celebrations. John had opened his snowcone stand for the second summer running. Jean had a part-time job, and Anne had enough to do simply keeping track of her family's varied schedules—meals staggered, friends and relatives coming and going. They weren't able to gather as a family as often as they would have liked, so when Marty and Joyce invited John out for an evening of talk, he was happy to join them.

They met at Mason's Bar. Marty and Joyce were already seated when John entered.

"John? Over here," Marty called.

"Hey, John, how's it going?" The bartender leaned over to snap his towel at John, grinning his welcome. "Haven't seen you all summer." A high school classmate of Marty, the bartender had known John for several years; and though he was only Martin's age he'd already begun to go bald. That, and sampling the food from the kitchen—which had brought him to thirty pounds over his high school weight—made him look several years older.

"Hey, Phil." John rubbed his own waist. "Putting on a little there, aren't you?"

"What have I got to lose it for? Betty likes me a little heavy."

"A little? You ought to get a T-shirt that says 'Goodyear' on it."

Jack and Lois Ryan, two friends at the far end of the mahogany bar, laughed. "Got you that time, Phil," Jack said.

"Uh-huh, sure. Wait'll he stops playing football, then see what happens to his weight."

"Not a chance!" John joined Marty and Joyce. "Been here long?"

Marty laughed. "Long enough to give Phil the same treatment you just gave him."

"He was just getting over Marty's kidding," Joyce said, "when you started in on him. Better keep an eye on him when he fixes a drink for us."

"I'll get it," Marty said, rising. "Are you still drinking . . . ?" When John nodded, he sighed and walked over to the bar.

"You've got a good tan," Joyce said.

"That's my day. I sit out there behind the stand, soaking up rays."

"Uh-huh. And playing catch with Joey." Joyce fiddled with the jukebox selector on the wall beside her. "We drove by yesterday and saw the two of you."

John turned to watch his brother loading a tray at the bar. The room was cool and dark. Above the mirror that stretched the length of the bar hung two signs —Schmidt's and Ortleib's—both in glowing, multicolored neon. Mason's was a family bar—an institution disappearing from cities like New York, Chicago and Philadelphia, except in the near suburbs or in certain South Philadelphia neighborhoods. Two-thirds restaurant, one-third social club, people came to Mason's on a hot night to meet friends over a hoagie or a steaming pizza and a pitcher of beer. And Mason's was one of the few bars left where you could get ice cream.

Marty exchanged a few words with the Ryans and came back with the tray. He set down a stein in front of Joyce, another at his place and held up a glass of soda and ice.

"Phil?" he called.

"Yeah?"

"Frisbee!" Marty yelled, and sailed the empty tray back to him, laughing as his friend snatched the spinning tray in mid-air. Then he slid into the booth beside Joyce, tapping her glass to say, "One beer. For me a beer. And for you"—handing the glass to John across the table—"one diet *yucccch!*"

"I hate it now," John admitted. "But I'll love it when Paterno sees my weight."

"You haven't put on any weight this summer," Joyce said.

"Four pounds."

"Four pounds? Is that all?"

"When he says come in at two-twelve," John told her, "he doesn't mean two-thirteen."

Marty said, "The few times I talked to Paterno, he didn't seem like a tyrant to me."

"He's not a tyrant. He just thinks we've got a chance for a terrific team this year."

"Him and me both," Marty said.

"So he expects everyone to give it the best shot possible."

Marty grew thoughtful. "I'm predicting . . . oh, say, ten-and-one this year."

"Oh come on. With our schedule?"

"I figure you'll get your hundred yards a game, and—"

"Joyce!" John interrupted in mock exasperation. "You ought to keep him locked up when he gets like this."

"It should be quite a fall," she said.

They sat and chatted over their drinks, now and then talking louder as the jukebox blared to life. It wasn't a crowded night. Neighborhood friends stopped in from time to time. On their way out the Ryans stopped to talk for a few minutes. The Wilcox family's oldest son voiced his prediction on the Penn State up-coming season. A couple of times Phil called out from the bar, asking John to settle some question of fact about Penn State. It was a pleasant evening and they all enjoyed themselves. But no matter what they talked about, the conversation always drifted back to the football season ahead. It wouldn't be long before John had to leave for training camp.

"I hope the folks can make it to all the home games," he said.

Marty shook his head in wonder. "Hey, you think the sun's going to rise in the east?"

"I'm talking about Joey," said John.

"You know Joey better than that," Joyce said. "Nothing's going to keep him away from a Penn State game."

John sat making rings on the tabletop with the base of his glass, then wiped them dry with his sleeve. "That's not necessarily true. It's obvious that the pain's getting worse."

"Yes, but he'd had—"

"Last week, when he was having trouble with his spleen, he couldn't even straighten up. The doctor said it was like an attack of appendicitis, only for Joey it lasted four days!"

"Uhhh."

"I'll tell you something else," John said. "A friend of mine at school had a spinal tap last spring. He was telling me afterward, he never felt pain like that in his life. Well, Joey's had one every month, for years."

"I know what you mean," Joyce said. "A girl I knew went through that, a spinal tap, I mean."

"And I've never heard Joey say it hurts," Marty added.

John was quiet but obviously troubled. "I don't see how he holds up. And Mom. I don't see how she holds up either."

Anne Cappelletti held up because she had to. It was no more complicated than that. She was determined that Joey wouldn't find out just how ill he really was, or how much she worried about him. She treated many of his ailments with what might have seemed to an outsider a casual attitude. It wasn't so much that she had grown accustomed to Joey's problem—that would never happen—as that she wanted to protect him from a knowledge that couldn't help him in any way.

When the Pee Wee League ended its season, Joey received a special award as the most courageous player in the league. He stood in line with the other Cardinals, beaming, and stepped forward to accept the team trophy that all his teammates were given. After the general awards had been called out, individual trophies went to the boy with the highest batting average, to the pitcher with the best won-lost record, and finally the special award to Joey. He accepted it with pleasure, and not a little bewilderment: he didn't consider what he'd done as "courageous," only necessary. In that, he was like his mother.

But his bewilderment was nothing compared to the curiosity his appearance raised in the parents attending the open-air ceremony. When Joey stepped up to accept the trophy, he was wearing a stocking cap—on a humid day with the temperature in the high eighties.

He wore that stocking cap—a black knit Navy watch-cap—most of the summer, because the new medication he'd been taking had caused his hair to fall out. The family' had grown accustomed to it, but to strangers Joey was a peculiar sight, especially on hot, muggy days when his stocking cap topped off a costume of shorts and T-shirt, as it did most of that summer.

On one visit to the hospital, Joey saw that Mark was already there. They no longer ran into each other every week, due to a shift in Joey's appointment schedule. When they did, they spent several minutes catching up on what had happened since they last met. Mark had never seen Joey in the watch-cap.

When Joey hopped onto the chair, Mark looked at the cap curiously and said, "Joey? Why have you got that thing on?"

Without saying a word, Joey pulled the woolen cap off. A mass of light brown waves spilled over his forehead. The hair that had grown back had changed his appearance radically. No longer black and straight, it was a light brown imitation of Shirley Temple's at her cutest.

Mark couldn't resist the impulse to reach up in awe to touch one of the curls. "Gee! How 'bout that."

"I hate it," Joey said, tugging the cap on again.

"Why?"

"The girls are always trying to feel it."

"Ugh!" Mark shared Joey's distaste.

"Yeah."

"Hey, Joey." Mark bounced in his chair with excitement. "Guess what?"

"What?"

"I may get to go to Disneyworld." And then, not to get his hopes too high, he added, "Maybe."

"That's terrific!"

"People are getting up . . . you know, this 'fund' they call it. And if they get enough money, they're going to send us to Disneyworld."

"Mark, the doctor's ready now." A nurse beckoned from down the corridor. "Will you come with me?"

Mark hopped down from his chair. Calling over his shoulder as he left, he said, "If we get to go, I'll send you a postcard."

That conversation stayed on Joey's mind. The next afternoon, as he sat on an upturned crate in the stand with John, his nose buried in a cherry snowcone, Joey told him all about it.

"Sounds like fun," John said. Busy serving two girls so small they had to stand on tiptoe at the window, he was listening with only half his attention.

"I guess these people are worried because Mark's been sick so much," Joey said. "He has the same trouble I do." He said it so casually that he might have been talking about a sore toe. "So they're going to send him. Isn't that something?"

John made change for the girls and turned around to look at his brother. Joey sat on the crate with his legs crossed, Indian-fashion, the stocking cap in place. And though the boy didn't seem upset by the project for Mark, John was edgy about the conversation. "That's great," he agreed. "But listen, Joey. You've been lots of places too, y'know."

Joey was puzzled. "What's that got to do with it?"

John slid his chair next to Joey. "I thought you were jealous because Mark was going and you weren't."

"No," Joey said impatiently. "I just want to help him, that's all."

"Oh." John considered how best to explain the problem Joey's generosity would cause. "Well, Joey, you know how hard Dad works, but it's expensive with a big family."

"I know that."

"And Dad can't afford just to give money away, even if he wants to."

There was no conniving in Joey's answer, only innocent surprise. "Dad already gave me twenty-five dollars."

"He did?"

"Uh-huh. So all I want from you is ten."

John stared at him for a moment, feeling a little like the victim of a holdup. He shook his head, turning to the cash box. He took out a five dollar bill and held it up, but Joey shook his head. John counted out five singles, added them to the five.

Joey stuffed the bills into his shirt pocket and returned to his snowcone.

"That's it," John joked. "No more free snowcones for you, Buster."

"Oh, hey, that's right. Thanks, John."

"Uh-huh. 'Thanks, John.' "

"No, I really mean it." Joey jumped off the crate and darted off.

"Now where are you off to?"

"Marty's coming over after work. I'm going to see

how much he'll give me. It costs a lot to go to Disneyworld."

17

Anne was getting John's clothes in shape for the
coming school year. She mended socks and shirts, and
sorted out those slacks he had outgrown that might be
put aside for Michael—though Mike was almost as
large as John—slowly accumulating two stacks of
clothes for her sons. Michael was also going away to
Penn State this fall, and getting both sons ready was
nearly a fulltime job.

The boys helped her. John gave Michael tips on
what he ought to be ready for, since he'd already been
through the sometimes shocking transition from high
school to college. He knew that the difference in the
caliber of football competition wouldn't be Michael's
biggest surprise. John also sorted through textbooks
he had brought home the preceding spring at the end
of his junior year. There were several that might be
useful.

"How 'bout bermudas?" Michael asked.

"Not unless you want to freeze your knees," John
told him. "Man, that's *snow* country in those mountains!"

"Aw, c'mon, John. You don't mean—"

"Have it your way. I'm just telling you. A pair of
jeans and all the notebooks and pencils you can carry,
that's all you'll need." He waved off his brother's doubts
and went downstairs.

He'd packed enough to last till the Thanksgiving
break, when the really cold weather would begin to
settle over State College. If he needed anything he'd
forgotten, the family would be up on football weekends.

He had just sat down at the kitchen table with a bowl of cereal when he heard a commotion in the living room. Joey was darting from one room to another and back again. Then Anne ran past.

"What's going on?" he called.

Joey had reappeared, his mother in hot pursuit. "Joey, I want it, and I want it *now!*" she said.

"But Richie gave it to me." Joey feinted left and went right, then feinted left . . . *and went left!* It was a move to match Dr. J. at his best, but Joey wasn't going one-on-one for the basket; he was keeping the big maple table between himself and his mother, holding a magazine safe behind his back.

"I don't care who gave it to you," Anne said. "You give it to *me!*"

Joey bolted away again. John caught a glimpse of the latest issue of *Playboy* as the youngster ran from the room, his mother hard on the chase.

"Richie was as mad as I was," Joey shouted. "I only want to show it to John."

"If John wants to see it he can wait till he's at school. Not here!"

Again Joey reappeared. He approached his brother. "John, look! I want to show you what this creepy—"

As he held out the magazine, Anne snatched it from him. "Now!" she said. She rolled it into a tight scroll and held it high overhead, out of Joey's reach.

"Awww, Mom. I wanted to show John."

John knew he was involved in the ruckus, but he didn't know *how* he was involved. "What is it?"

Anne held up the *Playboy*, keeping Joey behind her as she showed John the centerfold. "Would you look at what our ten-year-old is reading now?" she said. Then she slammed the magazine shut and held it out of reach, responding to John's quick grin. "You can laugh if you want to, but this is not for a boy of his age."

Joey, exasperated, slumped in the chair across from John. "The only reason Richie gave it to me was because John's picture isn't in it."

"I don't care what *isn't* in it," Anne said. "I saw plenty of what *is* in it!" She held the magazine in her tightly clenched fist and left the room.

"What?" Joey called after her. Then he realized what she meant. "Oh. Naked girls? Who cares about that?"

Through a chuckle, John said, "What's the trouble, Joey?"

Leaning forward, his elbows on the table, Joey grew serious, determined to explain himself. "Richie's brother bought it to look at your picture, you know? In their all-American team for next year? But your picture wasn't there!" Anne had returned.

"I could have told you that," said John.

With a quick doubletake from one to the other, Anne asked John pointedly, "How did *you* know?"

"I knew," John shrugged, completely nonchalant, "because nobody took my picture for the magazine."

"Oh."

"But why, John?" Joey asked. "The *Bulletin* says you're going to be all-American."

"The *Bulletin* says *maybe* I'm going to be all-American."

Joey made his pronouncement. "*I* think you're going to make it."

"Good," John said, happy that it was all settled. He returned to his cereal.

"Boy, are the people at that magazine going to feel dumb when you do." Bouncing to his feet, eyes alight, Joey said, "Hey! I know what!"

"What are you thinking now, young man?" said Anne, her mind still on *Playboy*.

"I know how John can fix them. He'll just go out and win the Hideman Trophy."

Automatically, John said, "Heisman," and kept on eating.

"You two," Anne said, and left the kitchen again.

"And when you win it, they'll really feel like a bunch of jerks."

John mulled over Joey's hunch. "Okay," he said. "As long as I don't have anything else to do this fall."

FALL 1973

18

While Michael was playing fullback on the Penn State freshman team, John was the starting tailback for the Lion varsity—and a marked man. Pre-season experts had picked Penn State to finish high in the national rankings, and football fans throughout the country watched with interest. It wasn't possible to see the Nittany Lions in action without also noticing their premiere runner, Number 22.

Even more interested than the fans were scouts from Penn State's scheduled opponents. They carried home reports that said, in simple language, *"Stop Cappelletti."* But their reports were unable to explain exactly how to do that. As fast as a new offense is born, new defenses spring up. When the Wishbone appeared, opposing teams spread two linebackers wider to contain the attack. Many N.F.L. teams assigned a linebacker or defensive back to move with O.J. when he went in motion behind the line, keying on him. But keying on Number 22 did little good, when he came straight at the defense; and pulling the linebackers inside to plug holes blown in the line by the Penn State blockers only opened the wings for wide sweeps around end. It wasn't a complicated offense that Penn State threw at its opponents. It was simply an offense that worked.

Over the years the great teams in football, teams coached by Woody Hayes at Ohio State, by Vince Lombardi in the glory years at Green Bay, by Joe Paterno in later years, shared a common trait. They differed in style, in personnel, in the emphasis placed on passing versus running the ball. They lacked the razzle-dazzle play of southwestern college teams or Houston and Dallas among the pros. What they had in common was execution. It's a word most coaches use:

"Execution." But the Hayes, Lombardi, and Paterno
teams did more than talk about it.

The Nittany Lions had no tradition of a particular
style of football. They did have a tradition of winning.
Joe Paterno's winning percentage was over 80—tops
among college coaches with more than five years in the
game. There was one good reason for his success:
Paterno's teams came out ready to play . . . without
flash, but with superb execution.

The scouts saw that in the earliest games of the
1973 season, and they saw something else—an offense
that might have been called "Cappelletti and an Occasional Pass." It was not that John was the only one
called upon to carry the ball. Fullbacks Tom Donchez
and Bob Nagle were there; Walt Addie filled in. But
in the toughest going it was John who bulled his way
through openings that closed too soon and ran over
linemen waiting for him but unable to stop his progress. He wasn't as fast as some, not a hip-weaving high-
stepper; all he had was the uncanny ability to stay on
his feet and keep going.

In those early games—victories over Stanford, Navy,
Ohio—John made incredible runs. Not long, not blind-
ingly fast, but simply evidenced determination to keep
going as he shook off tacklers the way a dog sheds
water. More like Jim Brown than any other great runner, he bounced off one defender, ran over others,
and when someone who'd been hanging onto his
broad shoulders finally brought him down, the tackler
could look back upfield to discover he'd literally been
carried for five or six yards. John didn't make many
long gains, just many gains—no 100-yard, record-set-
ting bursts, but scores of gains, five yards at a crack.

After Stanford was set down 20-6, came Navy. The
score in that game: Penn State 39, Navy 0. And then
came Iowa. In the third quarter John broke loose up
the middle for 22 yards, one of his best runs of the
day, only to fumble on the Iowa seven-yard line. The
fumble had no effect on the final outcome of the game
but it embarrassed him; it recalled several fumbled
punt returns during his sophomore year, and he had to

fear momentarily that he'd lapsed into the bad habit his junior year had conquered. He gritted his teeth and dug in, and though he didn't score in the fourth quarter he was a principal factor in Penn State's playing ball-control as they ground out a 27-8 victory in the rain before a Beaver Stadium Homecoming crowd. The Iowa Hawkeyes managed their lone score with only 1:36 remaining—against the Penn State reserves.

The locker room after the game was chaotic. It was Homecoming, with friends and family on hand, and the Lions had beaten a tough Iowa team decisively. Well-wishers joined the shouting players in the locker room, some wet from the shower, others still soaked and muddied from the game.

Joey Cappelletti was in the middle of it all. He was sitting on a trainer's table being lectured by an earnest Eddie O'Neill. "Y'see, Joey? That's the kind of stuff I've got to put up with all the time," O'Neill said.

"What?"

"The defense goes out there . . . and we dig in . . . and we fight . . . and we stop 'em . . . and we take the ball away."

"Right," Joey said.

"Right, and then your ham-handed brother comes in and fumbles!"

"Once! Just one time."

O'Neill looked up at the ceiling, pantomiming frustration at Joey's inability to see the simple truth. "Man, he gives that ball away like he's passing out Christmas presents!"

Joey bounced to his knees on the table, still shorter than O'Neill but more nearly able to look him in the eye. He was enjoying himself enormously. "O'Neill," he said. "You're such a turkey, you wouldn't know the Iowa goal line if you tripped over it."

O'Neill staggered back as if he'd been pole-axed, horrified at the insult. He mimed a few sobbing gasps and stumbled away while Joey laughed in delight.

Coach Paterno circled through the melee quietly, stopping now and then to congratulate and thank the players. He waved in response to shouted greetings and stopped beside John Cappelletti's locker. "Joey looks better than I've seen him in a long time," he said.

"Yeah," John agreed. "I think the way the team's been going, it's really got him high." He glanced at his brother's beaming face and recognized what good medicine the victory had been for the boy. "If we can only keep it up," he said.

Paterno dropped a hand on his shoulder. "I'll settle for that," he said dryly and walked off.

When Joey hopped down off the table to dart through the crowd to John's side, he nearly disappeared. Surrounded by young athletes two or three times his size, he seemed smaller than ever—a curly-haired sprite ducking between giants as if caught in a maze. And happier than ever. He bounded up to seize John's hand and pump it excitedly. "Boy! Is he going to be sorry he made that bet with me," Joey said.

John dropped to the bench in front of his locker and stripped his socks off to begin the task of cutting the tape from his ankles. "Who's going to be sorry?"

"Marty. Just wait."

"Joey, you lost me. I don't know what you're talking about."

"We had a bet about what the team was going to do this year. I bet him two shoeshines."

"Yeah?"

Joey laughed. "He said the team's going to be ten and one."

"And you argued with him? I thought you were one of our boosters."

"I am!" Joey said indignantly. "But how are you guys going to lose a game?"

John shook his head, grinning at his brother's confidence. "Coach?" he called out. "Do you want to come talk to this guy? Tell him who we've got on the schedule."

19

It had been a year since Joey's near-fatal bout with chicken pox, a year that had brought many changes to the Cappelletti home. Marty had already married and left the house, and John might as well have moved out, considering how busy his work at Penn State kept him, in the classroom and on the gridiron. Now Michael's bed was empty, too, and Joey was the last son still at home.

There had been physical changes in Joey himself. He was taller now, and heavier. He'd regained the weight lost in the hospital and it was good, solid weight, not the artificial puffiness that appears as one side effect of medications, like Prednisone, that Joey had been taking. His leukemia was in remission, the sessions of risky chemotherapy at an end . . . For how long, no one could say with any certainty. To all outward appearances he looked like a healthy, normal, curly-haired boy of ten. Those curls were the most visible change of all.

But one fact of his life hadn't changed: Saturday and its excitement was the day he lived for, no matter how depressed he might become during the rest of the week. Joey seemed to husband his strength throughout the week and then on weekends to exhaust himself in a flurry of activity. In his imagination he felt every blow John took on the field. Seated in Beaver Stadium, identifying with his brother, he lurched when John cut back against the flow or slammed over a would-be tackler. He participated so much in John's every move that he came home from those Saturdays tired at best, occasionally near exhaustion, his enthusiasm spent. It took most of the following week for that enthusiasm to build again.

On Monday, the low point of Joey's week, he sat

on the window seat staring out the bay window. Jean entered, tugging on her sweater. Now that Michael was gone she was the only one living at home with Joey besides their parents, and she was taking on more and more responsibility for him. She usually stayed in the background and said little to Joey, but there was not much she missed.

"Joey," she said.

He didn't even glance her way.

"Hey, Joey. You want to play rummy till the bus comes?"

He swung around on the window seat and looked at her listlessly. "I guess not," he said.

"Sure. Something else, then?"

He seemed to be looking past her into the kitchen, or through her, as if she weren't even in the room with him. "Nothing."

"What's the matter today, Joey?"

"Nothing." He blinked quickly. "Will you just let me alone?" he snapped. He went past her to the table where his school books lay to pick them up, looking at them as if they belonged to someone else.

Outside, a horn blew. Anne Cappelletti appeared in the doorway. "Joey," she said. "There's the bus."

"I hear it." He wouldn't look at his mother either.

"Now don't forget and take the bus home today. I'll pick you up and we'll go to the hospital right from school."

"Don't bother," he said. He walked toward the front door.

"What?"

Joey's voice was fierce. "Don't bother, 'cause I'm not going to be there!" He slammed the door behind him as he left.

Anne and Jean watched him stalk down the sidewalk. His attempt at bravado didn't last long. Halfway to the bus, his stride lost its vigor and he slouched.

"Do you know what that's about?" asked Jean.

Anne shook her head.

"He's sure cranky today."

"Never mind," Anne said. "You run along, or you'll

be late." She smiled with more confidence than she felt and watched as Jean gathered up her own books and left.

Joey's illness was a constant concern. Each day brought both the promise of continued remission of the disease and the increasing possibility that it might flare up again as his body developed resistance to the drugs that helped keep the leukemia in check. Failing that, he might at any time develop harmful side effects from those very drugs. Knowing all that, she had to keep in mind that Joey was one of five children. Anne also knew it would have been easy to spoil him and to lavish all her attention on him.

She and John Sr. had discussed the situation over and over again. Neither of them wanted that, and they corrected one another when the possibility loomed large. The other children never spoke of any extra attention to Joey. They felt as their parents did— that Joey needed and deserved their love. Martin, John, Michael, Jean, all of them learned selflessness without even considering that the way they behaved toward Joey and one another might be anything extraordinary. They were mutually concerned with one another, contributing to and drawing from their shared love in equal measure.

Joey was but one figure in the total equation. Keeping that equation in balance, Anne felt, was a function that belonged to her. She was the center of their home life, just as John Sr. could be regarded as the center of quiet strength in their lives outside the home. The two complemented each other perfectly. And neither of them seemed to know how much neighbors and friends admired them for the shape they had given their lives.

During those quiet days at home, Anne had the chance to reflect on the patterns their lives had assumed in recent years. She wasn't depressed. She felt contentment in the stable situation she and her husband had arranged. Joey's uncertain future was an unavoidable cloud on the horizon, but not a cloud over her features. She went through the daily routine gratefully, cheerfully, the same woman she might have been if all her children had been completely healthy. And that trait, her warm equanimity, was what her children valued and her friends singled out as the essential quality of the Cappelletti family. "They're . . . I don't know . . . 'nice' people," their neighbors would say. "They're always happy."

But the cloud remained in the horizon. And on that Monday afternoon, driving to pick up Joey at school, Anne was apprehensive. Joey's flare-up that morning, the anger he'd shown, had made her edgy. Throughout Joey's long struggle with leukemia, the various medications given him in the experimental program had caused minor personality changes in him at unexpected times. There had been bouts of nausea and frightening lethargy. Once a prescribed drug intended to enable him to sleep had in fact produced the opposite result: Joey had spent most of the night talking, singing, brimming with energy. Anne had reported the effect of the drug and Joey's doctors immediately changed his prescription.

Driving along, Anne worried that Joey's flare of temper might be evidence of some flaw in the treatment he was receiving, or—worse yet—an indication that his condition was about to take an unforeseen turn. As stable as his condition had been in recent weeks, any turn could only be a turn for the worse.

When she arrived at his school, Joey was nowhere in sight. She didn't overreact, but pulled the car to the curb to wait.

A few minutes went by.

Still no Joey.

She had opened the door to get out when she caught a glimpse of him sitting just beyond a large oak tree at the corner of the schoolyard. She closed the car door quietly so that Joey wouldn't hear and waited.

Soon, Joey rose wearily, crossed the lawn and got into the car.

She pulled the car out into traffic. "How was your day?" she asked, her voice consciously neutral.

"Okay."

"Did you remember to hand in your homework?"

"Ummm."

"Take a look in the bag." She tapped the brown paper bag on the seat between them. "I brought you some cookies to eat on the way."

"I don't want any."

Anne took a deep breath, gripped the steering wheel with both hands as if it were alive and trying to escape. "All right, what are you mad about?"

"Why do I have to go to the hospital when I'm not sick?"

"Joey, we've been through this—"

"Why?"

Quietly, Anne explained as she'd done so many times before. "So you'll go on feeling well. Your Dad doesn't wait till the car breaks down before he has a checkup, does he?"

"Boy! When I get over this, I'm never going near a hospital again!"

Anne stopped the car at a traffic light, fighting her own emotions. To hear Joey talk about getting "over this" was nearly more than she could take, but practice had given her the knack of sounding casual even in the most strained moments. She said simply, "Okay. But for now, let's try to do what the doctor says."

His head turned away from his mother, Joey stared out the window. "Can't even go to the game this week," he muttered.

"Joey, it's too far. The Air Force Academy is clear out in Colorado."

It wasn't an answer he would accept, not in the mood he was in just then. His dogged reaction reminded his mother of how young he really was: "Why does Colorado have to be so far from here?"

The second question she couldn't answer in two minutes, but this was the normal sort of "why?" that many children blurt out in response to any answer given them. She said, "The team will be back next weekend, Joey. In time for your birthday."

He looked up at her suspiciously, as if to check her motive. Was she only trying to cheer him up? He couldn't decide, and wasn't light-hearted enough to voice an answer, but the smile that sneaked unbidden across his face was response enough.

20

A folktale from India describes three blind men coming upon an elephant for the first time and then exchanging descriptions of what they had found. One grasped a tusk and defined the animal as a polished tree limb. Another seized the tail and decided that an elephant must be very much like a snake. The third man, who'd run his hands along the elephant's side, argued that it must certainly resemble a leather wall. Penn State's head trainer, Chuck Medlar, had a staff of assistants whose daily contact with the Lions gave them a view of each player nearly as distorted as those of the three blind men.

At the foot of a padded table, football trainers tape dozens of ankles one after another. A trainer gets to recognize each player by the shape and appearance of his ankles—bruised, hairless, freckled, bony, or broken.

As each player sits on the table, the trainer tears strips of adhesive tape—from a roll held in his teeth or tucked under his chin—and with both hands tapes the ankle before him, so rapidly that an observer can hardly follow the steps of the process. When he reaches up to slap the leg, the tape-supported foot swings out of sight to be replaced by another. Preventive medicine by Henry Ford.

John waited on the assembly line beside Joey. They were talking. When the man ahead of him left the trainer's table, John jumped on.

"Is West Virginia a good team?" Joey asked.

"They're all good teams when they play us," John said.

"But you're going to beat them, aren't you?"

"I'll tell you that in about four hours."

Joey chattered, half his attention on the trainer's flashing hands.

Eddie O'Neill passed by, his ankles already taped. He wore his pants and his pads, over an undershirt, but no jersey. "We got to put somebody on the door," he said. "They're letting kids in here now. Little bitty kids in the locker room!"

Joey looked up and smiled.

O'Neill ignored him and walked on, muttering, "Kids, little kids, little tiny kids."

Joey basked in the warmth of being beside John, a part of all the pre-game activity in the Penn State locker room. He could name every piece of John's equipment. He knew that too firm a support to the ankle throws stresses to the knee—most vulnerable in a running back. He could describe the different shoes used by the players: cleats, of course, but also rubber ripple-soles for frozen field conditions; the square-toed kicker's shoe; the high-cut linemen's shoes and some low-cuts favored by a few of the backs (and none of the trainers). O'Neill's jibes warmed him even more. He was welcome, and knew enough to enjoy that feeling without getting in the way.

He stood now beside the trainer, where John could see him without turning his head, making certain of keeping his brother's attention. "Did I tell you about Mark's dog?"

"I don't think so." John reached down to smooth the layered tape on his left ankle, while the trainer shifted to his right. "What dog are you talking about?"

"They had some money left over from the trip."

"Oh, how was the trip?" John asked. "What did he think of Disneyworld?"

"Great! When you come home I'll show you the card he sent me. But anyway, they took the money they had left over, and they bought Mark a dog."

John reached down to test the other ankle. "Sounds like a good idea."

"And it was chasing a rabbit," Joey said. "And the rabbit bit him."

John's head snapped up. "Oh, come on, Joey."

"It did, John! It's just a little bitty dog."

John laughed and swung his feet to the side as the trainer slapped his leg. He hopped off the table.

"Hey. You know what's the best part of this weekend?" Joey asked.

"What?" John led the way to his locker. "Come on over here. I want to get my socks."

"You're coming home with us."

"I wouldn't want to miss your birthday party." John sat on the bench in front of his locker and pulled on a pair of white cotton socks. His motions were automatic; he was able to dress quickly without losing track of Joey's comments.

"I'm really glad, John."

"Me too. The only thing is, your present may be a little late. I've really had a busy week." He took his jersey from the locker.

"That's okay," Joey said.

John's head popped out of the blue jersey like a turtle from its shell. "What would you like?"

"I don't know."

"Come on, give a guy a hint."

"Hey, yeah!" His eyes alight, Joey scampered in front of John. "I know something."

John tugged the shirt loose under his arms, tucking it in around his hip pads to make certain it was snug and comfortable. "Go ahead," he said. "Fire away."

"I'd like three touchdowns. No, four."

"When?" John asked.

"Today."

After a moment's thought, John nodded. "Well, I guess there's a chance we could score four against them." He thumped Joey on the shoulder. "You got it."

Joey said, "I mean you, John."

"Me?" John's head snapped up. "What are you

talking about? I've never scored four touchdowns in one game in my life! And not many other people have, either."

Joey looked up at him with absolute trust. "You asked me what I wanted."

"I know, but—"

"And this way you don't have to go shopping or anything."

"Yeah, Hoss, but—"

"Joey?" Dad's voice interrupted as he approached them. "Come on. We're going to get something to eat before the game starts."

Joining his father, Joey turned back to wait for John's answer. "Well?"

John stood, one foot on the bench, and studied Joey. Then he sighed. "Okay."

"*Thanks*, John." As if the present had already been wrapped and delivered.

John watched them go, shaking his head. How could he have been foolish enough to make such a promise? When he turned back to his locker, Eddie O'Neill stood there behind him, a smirk on his face. Uncertain how much O'Neill had heard, and unwilling to discuss the whole conversation, John stepped past him to reach into his locker.

O'Neill wouldn't be diverted. He tapped John on the shoulder. "You saw the late show too, huh?"

"What do you mean?"

O'Neill's eyes were guileless. "You got it a little mixed up, though."

"What are you talking about, O'Neill?"

The soul of sweet reason, Eddie said, "Listen. When Gary Cooper promised the kid he'd hit two home runs, it was because Babe Ruth had already promised him one. I mean, did you have to *start out* offering four?"

"I didn't start out offering *anything*. He was the one who . . ." John's voice trailed off. It was useless to fight O'Neill's needling; he shook his head and turned to the locker. When he didn't hear O'Neill's footsteps departing, he glanced back over his shoulder.

O'Neill still stood there, four fingers held up, silently mouthing the question: *"Four?"*

Throughout the pre-game warmup John returned in his imagination to the expression on Joey's face, to the satisfaction Joey had shown for a present he was absolutely confident of getting. More and more John regretted his rash agreement. But regret couldn't retract his promise.

The game started and John didn't waste any time. He blasted over right tackle from the West Virginia ten to score the first touchdown of the day.

The cheering from more than 59,000 fans at Beaver Stadium was all any Lion booster could ask for, but in the midst of that screaming crowd sat one silent ten-year-old. Joey was absolutely calm, the only sign of his pleasure a somewhat self-satisfied smile. As others around him leaped to their feet, Joey sat with his arms folded, his right hand lying on his left arm, the index finger extended. That was number one.

The second one was easy—or may have looked that way from the stands. Center Rich Caravella blew a hole in the West Virginia defensive line and John rode the wake of Caravella's block into the end zone

Again the stands erupted, especially the Cappellettis. Joyce hugged Marty as Michael threatened their eardrums with his shrill piercing whistle. It was their John down there. Two scores already. Two Penn State touchdowns in a game only a few minutes old.

Still Joey just sat there. Now his right hand showed two extended fingers.

Some ten minutes into the game Number 22 scored again. The play was a quick-opener, Cappelletti off left guard. Tom Shuman's handoff slammed into his belly and John hit the hole just as a linebacker closed it, bounced off the defender and spun left to take it in with a halfback clutching uselessly at his arm. *Three* touchdowns.

The stands were pandemonium. Few people there had ever seen a running exhibition like that—and the game was still young. Only Joey was quiet, the third finger on his right hand proudly erect. Why should he join the screaming frenzy? He had secret, inside information.

Number four in the private contract between John and Joey should have been a cinch: Penn State, first-and-goal on the West Virginia three. But a mixup in the Lion backfield found John a half-step early—or the quarterback slow in his spin—and the handoff missed, the ball popped into the air and West Virginia covered the fumble. The sudden turn gave West Virginia a new strength and they recovered from the three stunning Penn State scores to begin a march of their own out of trouble. They had made one first down and were driving toward a second when on third-and-five the Mountaineers quarterback rolled to his right on an option play. Before he could commit himself to tuck the ball under his arm and try running the sidelines, or locate a receiver not covered by the Penn State defensive secondary, the blitzing Eddie O'Neill was on him. Williams hurried his throw and the ball wobbled through the air like a wounded duck to fall yards short of any possible receiver. Fourth-and-five, and West Virginia dropped back into punt formation.

On the sidelines the Penn State offensive unit jumped to their feet again, donning helmets. They were frantic with eagerness to get back onto the field.

"Cappy!" It was the voice of Coach Paterno.

John side-stepped his way through the knot of players bunched in front of the bench.

Paterno had to shout over the noise of the crowd. "You had a good workout. We'll let Walt get some experience now." He turned to yell, "Addie! You're in!"

Walt Addie came off the bench like a man shot from a cannon. For most college teams he'd have been starting at tailback, rather than spending his time on the bench awaiting his chance. He tugged his chin strap tight and sprinted onto the field to catch the rest of the offensive unit already forming their huddle.

The defense came off slapping hands with one another. Some slumped to the bench while others paced the sidelines to watch the offensive unit take over. John was clearly stricken by Paterno's decision. On most days he welcomed a breather and was glad to see Addie get the chance to add to the over 300 yards Walt had already accumulated that season. But this wasn't one of those days. He started toward the bench, hesitated, then decided to speak to Paterno. He walked back to the coach who was intent on the action on the field. John stood at his shoulder for a moment, unable to say anything. His own personal pledges couldn't dictate Paterno's actions. His shoulders slumped, he walked back to sit down.

In the excitement of the quick turnover of the ball and the possibility of the Lions scoring yet a fourth touchdown, not many fans noticed that John wasn't on the field. Walt Addie's family did, cheering for Walt, and so did the Cappellettis. It was Joey who was most concerned.

"Hey!" he shouted to his father. "John's not playing."

Anne leaned closer to her husband to make herself heard. "Do you think he's been hurt?"

"He's not hurt. With this kind of lead, Paterno's giving him a rest, that's all."

"He deserves it," Michael said. He knew what he was talking about. As fullback on the freshman team, he'd picked up his own share of bruises. He could appreciate how John must feel.

But Michael's reassurance didn't do much for Joey. Someone was trying to take his present away from him. He scowled down at the field.

Defensive Co-Captain Eddie O'Neill stood in the midst of his teammates on the sidelines watching the action on the field. Out of the corner of his eye he caught a glimpse of an assistant trainer passing behind him, carrying a rack of water bottles. Reaching for one of them, he spotted a glum John Cappelletti sitting alone on the bench.

O'Neill was the only person in the stadium who could read John's thoughts.

"Did you want some water, O'Neill?" The trainer was speaking.

"What? Oh, never mind." Eddie waved him away and trotted over to where Coach Paterno and one of his assistant coaches—wearing a headset—were conferring.

"Tell him we'll try it," Paterno said and turned away, as his assistant relayed the message to a spotter atop the press box on the west side of the stadium. "You want to see me?" he asked O'Neill.

Eddie bent down to speak quietly. His comments were inaudible to people standing nearby.

The coach's eyes opened wide. "You've gotta be kidding!" he said. He scanned the sidelines and located John still sitting alone on the bench.

Eddie shrugged. He had told the coach what he knew. That was all he could do. The rest was out of his hands.

John watched their huddled conversation. He saw Paterno looking at him. Paterno and O'Neill exchanged another comment. Then the coach was staring at John again, shaking his head.

John tapped himself on the chest, a question in his eyes.

"*Cappy!*" Paterno yelled.

John leaped to his feet and ran to Paterno's side.

The coach looked at him in consternation. Then, with a shrug, he said, "Okay. All right. Go on back in."

John clapped on his helmet and raced onto the field.

As the familiar Number 22 sprinted toward the huddle, a fresh cheer burst from the crowd.

Anne, watching his re-entrance into the game, said, "It wasn't much of a rest."

Joey smiled with quiet satisfaction, glancing down at the three extended fingers pressed against his coatsleeve.

Later, John would claim that his first three touchdowns had been luck—the breaks of being in the right place at the right time. Perfect blocking from his teammates. An accident. But not even he would claim that for what happened next. Because when he got back into the game, he was determined that it would take a dozen tanks to keep him out of that end zone. And as far as he knew, the Mountaineers didn't have any tanks in their defensive secondary.

Penn State marched the ball down to within two yards of the West Virginia goal line. On any one of those plays fullback Bob Nagle or Number 22 might have broken free to score. But they didn't. The actual score came on what Sunday's newspapers would blandly call a two-yard plunge. Only two yards in distance covered, it was a thousand miles in determination, because John Cappelletti hit the line after the hole had closed and both defensive tackle and linebacker were massing there to meet him. They hit him low but he crashed back into them, legs churning as he drove with irrational strength, carrying both of them into the end zone with him—where he slammed to the turf with a bone-rattling thud and the happiest, most satisfied feeling of his life.

"*Four* of 'em," Marty shouted. I don't *believe* it!"

Joey only smiled—and extended the fourth finger.

John ran to the sidelines grinning broadly. Teammates slapped his outstretched palms. Ducking away from the barrage of fists thumping his shoulder pads, he nearly bowled over Coach Paterno. He swerved to one side in time, and stopped abruptly. His grin turned sheepish.

Paterno debated the proper reaction. But the debate didn't last long. He smiled, slapping John on the shoulder pads.

John went to the water wagon. He nearly floated. Euphoric, as proud as he'd ever been, he seized one of the plastic bottles with its flexible plastic straw and sprayed a cooling draught down his throat.

Eddie O'Neill gently tapped his shoulder. "I don't know," he said. "Somehow Gary Cooper had more . . . *flair*. Y'know?"

John squirted water in O'Neill's grinning face. Then

his eyes searched the cheering crowd for the face of Joey.

Joey had watched Number 22 come off the field, and followed his trek to the water wagon, not taking his eyes off his brother for a second. In fact he'd missed two of West Virginia's plays, waiting to see how John would cap off the moment the two of them were privately sharing—in the midst of nearly 60,000 unknowing spectators. When John's head came around, and Joey saw him looking in his direction, Joey stood up to yell in his loudest voice: "Thanks for my present, John!"

21

"Jean, save the bows, will you?" Joyce was helping her sister-in-law clear away all the debris left in the wake of Joey's whirlwind passage through his piled-up birthday gifts.

"This one's got the stickum all gone," Jean said.

"Save it anyway. I'll be able to use it."

John was marveling in mock-wonder. "Would you look at all the loot!" he said. "Joey, I think you can open your own toy store."

On the floor lay a new baseball glove—Dad's present to Joey—a sweater his mother had knitted for him, games, a check from one of his aunts, and several birthday cards as yet unopened. In the Cappelletti household, birthdays were big events through the eleventh or twelfth. Then they diminished in importance, the real knockout celebrations resurrected for only two more birthdays, the sixteenth and the twenty-first. This had been Joey's eleventh, the last of his "childhood," and the family had made a real event of it, right down to Joey's favorite chocolate cake with chocolate icing.

Joey was about to open his last present.

"Who's it from?" Anne asked.

"I don't know." He tore at the silver wrapping, too eager to bother with the nonsense of carefully untaping the corners.

"There's a card there," Jean told him.

It took some will power but Joey laid down the package—with a sigh he thought he had coming—and opened the envelope to satisfy his mother's curiosity; his own curiosity was focused on the package at his feet. "Hey, look!" He waved the card. "It's from Coach Paterno." He threw the card toward his mother and dropped to his knees to rip open the package. Inside was a scale-model Penn State football jersey, just big enough for someone newly turned eleven, navy blue, with the white numerals 22 on the back below the name "CAPPELLETTI." "Wow! Look at this!"

There were hoots of enthusiasm. Marty said, "Hey, John—your number."

John pretended irritation at the gift. "Come on," he said. "I had that number first."

"Let's see how it fits." Michael took the jersey from Joey, stretched it across Joey's back and stepped away to arm's length, looking critically. "Good thing you've got a set of shoulders on you, Hoss, or they couldn't get 'Cappelletti' across it. They'd have to put 'Cap,' and then 'continued on next player.' "

"Let me have it," Joey said. He took it from Michael's hands and tugged it on over his shirt.

"Like a glove," John said, returning Joey's pleased grin.

Searching through the pile of wrapping paper, Jean asked, "Is that the end?"

"I think it's enough," Anne said. "Anybody for more cake?"

Everyone groaned their no's. Michael knelt to help clear away the debris.

With one hand Joey rubbed his shoulder, stroking the jersey, while his other hand stifled a yawn. "I'm a little tired," he said.

His father feigned a yawn of his own and said, "It's been a big weekend."

"Yeah, it really was. Maybe I'll just go up to bed." Joey kissed his father and mother and walked to the stairs, waving and calling, "Good night. Thanks for everything."

"Good night, Joey."

"Sleep well, Hoss."

As they returned to straightening the room, Dad motioned Michael toward him. "Mike, will you take these games out to the den?"

Joey had stopped motionless at the foot of the staircase. He was looking up. The way he was staring at them, the steps might have been a mountain.

Anne said, "Joey. Remember to write Coach Paterno and thank him, now don't forget."

"Okay." Joey rested one hand on the banister, lifted a foot to the first step, and then leaned his other hand on his knee to support himself.

John, who had watched his brother without saying anything, walked up to him and casually asked, "Want a lift? I'm going up myself."

"I am pretty tired," Joey admitted.

"Nothing to it." John picked him up easily and carried him upstairs to his room. "Anything wrong with that service?" John asked, dropping Joey lightly to the bed.

"Thanks, John." Joey wasn't in a joking mood.

"Okay then, Hoss. See you in the morning." John started to leave.

"John?"

"Yeah?" He stopped in the doorway to look back.

Joey lay on his bed, his head propped on one hand, and looked up at John with a somber expression. "Could I ask you something?"

John sensed that the question was serious, that Joey wasn't playing at all. "Sure," he said.

"Well, I know Mom or Dad would tell me if I asked them, but I'd rather ask you."

"Okay. Ask away."

"Do I have leukemia?"

The question hit John like a fist between the eyes. He fought to maintain a poker face as a sense of devastation flooded through him. His legs lost their strength. He rested one hand on the doorframe, grateful for the support.

The family had agreed always to answer Joey's questions truthfully, but only what he'd asked—no more. The time had come. With Joey's trusting gaze on him, he had no choice. John said simply, "Yes." Then he waited for what would follow.

Joey considered the answer solemnly. Then he nodded, his suspicions confirmed. When he looked up at John, he said, "I really liked my birthday present. The one you gave me."

Braced for an onslaught of unanswerable questions, John was thrown off-balance. Forcing a smile he didn't feel, he said, "I was pretty happy with it myself."

"I know I shouldn't ask you this, but . . ."

"Go ahead." Nothing Joey could say now would topple him.

"Well . . ." Joey hesitated, then blurted out, "Would you do it again for me next Saturday?"

"Would I . . . ?" The question absolutely flabbergasted him. He still hadn't recovered from the chill Joey's first question had given him. Nor was he certain that Joey now understood anything more about his affliction than a name, "leukemia." Did he understand the implications associated with that word? Nothing was apparent in the young boy's eyes but trust.

Unable to speak, John could only nod his agreement. Somehow, he would have to try.

22

In the past few years, the word "high" has taken on new meanings. Young people—and old—experiment with all sorts of stimulants, searching for a special high. But there is one that is often overlooked.

When John Cappelletti stepped onto the field at Beaver Stadium for the game against Ohio University, he was *high* . . . on determination alone. He had always played to win, and no one who'd ever seen him on the field—whether in his high school days at Monsignor Bonner High, in summer baseball leagues, or at Penn State—could accuse him of lacking concentration or giving less than his best. But on that November Saturday, John's concentration was incredible.

Before the game, he joined the jostling melee of players as they worked their energy to the point of near frenzy for the kickoff. But even then a part of him stayed withdrawn—cool, isolated, steady, watching himself at work. And when the game began, John was ready.

On Penn State's first possession of the ball they ground out yardage in the trenches, right down the middle. It was thudding, slamming, hard-driving work through the center of the line, with Donchez and Cappelletti carrying the ball. Taped fists and padded forearms slammed into them; linemen grunted in exertion —and in pain. Then, relentlessly, they pushed Ohio University back and back until John was able to score, taking it over from the one-yard line.

Within moments, the Lions were back on the attack. Their second touchdown was similar—not flashy, but effective. The Penn State linemen exploded out of a crouch and crashed into the Bobcat defenders to drive them erect, and back, and separate them. John found the holes, sliding along the line to cut back for daylight and pick up five and six and seven yards at a crack, until he finally bulled in his second touchdown. When the quarter ended, the score was Penn State 14, Ohio 7.

In the second quarter John broke free for his longest run of the day. From 25 yards out he circled left, cut inside the end, who threw a vicious block on the Ohio linebacker coming up, angled back for the center of the field, and with one jigging step faked his way past the defensive halfback till only the safety stood between him and the goal line. The safety, who had the angle on him, caught him from the side at the 5-yard line, and rode John Cappelletti's back into the end zone for touchdown number three.

Chris Bahr kicked his third extra point of the day.

Five minutes later, John broke free for another one, this time from the Ohio 15, thundering in for his second 12-point quarter and his fourth touchdown of the day. At halftime, according to Joey's tabulation, the score was John Cappelletti 28, Ohio 7.

The Band Day crowd had already gone crazy with John's third TD. With his fourth, pandemonium broke out. Brian Walsh was on his hands in his lion costume, pumping out 28 pushups to the cadenced screaming of the fans, while Joey wore a grin that christened every pushup.

John didn't score again for the rest of the game, but he continued to slash his way through the Bobcat defense. And when the day had ended, he'd picked up a total of 204 yards. The Nittany Lions whipped a game but outclassed Ohio team before a crowd of 51,804 screaming partisans at Beaver Stadium. As icing on Joey's cake, his buddy Ed O'Neill had picked off an Ohio pass and rambled 66 yards with the interception for a score of his own. Chris Bahr kicked seven extra points that day, four after John's touchdowns, a fifth after O'Neill's exciting run, another following a blocked punt return by linebacker Tom Hull, who ran 29 yards with the crowd's roar at his back to urge him on, and the last one after an 18-yard scoring sprint by Walt Addie. Number 22 didn't get back into this game. He sat on the bench, pleased at Addie's getting the well-deserved chance to score his second TD of the season.

With so many Lions involved in the scoring, with the score and victory so decisive, the locker room after the game was predictably bedlam. John was surrounded by reporters and TV cameras as Joey stood aside waiting patiently for his turn at John's attention.

One reporter, holding up a microphone, shouted over the din. "After you carried thirty-four times against Air Force, their coach, Ben Martin, was quoted as saying, 'Cappelletti didn't look tired at all. He could have played for another hour and a half.' How do you feel today?"

"Tired."

"You don't look it."

"I don't know how I look. That's how I feel."

"Do you think this victory—you're still undefeated now—do you think this victory will make Penn State number one?"

"I don't have any way of knowing that," John said.

"Okay, but do *you* think the team's number one?" the reporter persisted.

"I don't know that either." John laughed. "Right now all I know is, anybody that beats us is going to be an awfully good football team."

"Thanks, Cappy." The reporter turned and signaled for the cameraman to cut the lights on his portable shoulder-pack camera.

"Sure," John said, relieved to have the lights—and the reporter—gone.

As the newsmen crossed the room to interview Eddie O'Neill, John began to shed his uniform. He grinned at Joey who had walked up beside him. "Were you listening?" he asked. "What do you think? Are we number one?"

"You bet!" Joey said.

"I should have had them interview you."

Joey stood looking at the floor for a moment. When his gaze rose to meet John's, he said, "John?" He paused, the question in his eyes. "I don't suppose you could . . ." There was no need to finish the question.

John was flabbergasted. Two games were *enough!* He balled up his jersey and threw it at Joey, shouting, "Forget it! *Forget* it!"

John had no more four-touchdown games that season. Against North Carolina State, in a game that Penn

State won 35–29, he scored only three times—but one of those three proved to be the winning touchdown. His final score of the day was a 27-yard twisting, squirming run, which broke a 29–29 tie and put Penn State on top to stay.

Earlier in the game he had run one in from 34 yards out, another from the 8-yard line. As cold statistics in the newspapers, those two longer runs—27 and 34 yards—might have looked like the kind of figures a fan would expect from Bob Hayes of Dallas, the game-breaking sprinter. That wasn't the case with John. He'd covered 34 yards, right enough, including one stretch of nearly 10 yards without a hand being laid on him. But for much of that run he'd been hit, spun around, thrown back—and still he kept his feet. At least five N.C. State tacklers had a shot at him, but none could stop him. They bounced off his rolling, stocky body as he plowed through the defense, the goal line in sight, his sheer determination not to quit keeping him on his feet.

And though it wasn't a four-touchdown game, it was one of three consecutive games in which John gained over 200 yards. That day he set a school record by carrying the ball 41 times, on his way to a total of 220 yards gained!

Penn State closed out the season with a 35–13 victory over Pittsburgh. The Lion defense held Pitt to minus 15 yards of total offense in the third quarter. And the offense, led by John Cappelletti, tallied 32 unanswered points in the second half to complete Penn State's first 11-0 season. A crowd of 56,600 watched Penn State pour on 24 points in the final quarter. John ran one in from the 5; linebacker Tom Hull returned an intercepted pass for 27 yards and a score. Quarterback Shuman hit Chuck Herd with a 32-yard scoring pass, and Chris Bahr finished the scoring—and the 1973 season—with a 45-yard field goal.

For John it had been quite a year. In 11 games he had scored 17 touchdowns and gained 1,573 yards. His career totals were all the more impressive considering the fact that he had amassed them in only two

years as an offensive player: 2,639 yards gained in
519 carries—an average of 5.1 yards per rush. He
had averaged 120 yards per game. His total number of
touchdowns in two years: 29.

Every game of John's career was detailed in a bulg-
ing scrapbook Joyce had been keeping. Evenings, Joey
pored over the scrapbook, reading items pasted in during the preceding seasons, helping Joyce to add new
ones as they appeared in the newspapers. After Penn
State's undefeated season, more honors began to roll
in. Joey kept track of those, too.

John was chosen for the American football coaches'
all-American team; for all-American teams voted by
Football News, Sporting News, the Walter Camp Football Foundation, A.P., U.P.I., the Newspaper Enter-
prises Association, and *Time* magazine. If there was
an all-American team he *didn't* make, Joey Cappelletti
couldn't find a record of it.

23

"The Associated Press, on the basis of recommenda-
tions from its member newspapers, radio and television
stations, and reports from regional representatives, has
selected John Cappelletti, Penn State, first team running
back, a member of the all-American football team."

Marty read aloud from the brass-mounted wooden
plaque, then reached up to hang it on the nail he'd
driven into the wall of the paneled den. He had an appreciative audience: his father stood a few feet away,
hands on his hips, surveying the plaque and its center
position on the wall. Jean and Joyce sat on the couch.

"Looks good," Joyce said.

"It's the one we didn't have, anyway," Jean added.

And that was true. But the plaque, handsome as it
was, didn't actually outshine the many other trophies
and awards in the Cappelletti den. What gave it such

distinctive character was something other than mere appearance. Voted by hundreds of sports writers, it represented the accolades of men and women whose business it was to understand and value football, among other sports. They were authorities, they took their voting responsibilities seriously. And now, with Penn State having finished an undefeated season—thanks in part to John Cappelletti's success—some sports writers were saying that John had an outside chance to win the biggest honor of them all, the Heisman Trophy.

"Wouldn't that be neat?" Jean asked, hugging herself in a shiver of anticipation.

"I'm not saying he shouldn't win it," said Marty. "I'm just saying he won't."

"Supper!" Anne called from the kitchen.

"How can you be so sure of that?" Jean asked.

They went to the dining room.

"Smells good. What is it?" Dad said.

"You're worse than the kids," Anne said. "If you'll sit down, you'll find out."

Joyce was as puzzled by Marty's comment as Jean. "Why not? If his record is clearly the best, he ought to—"

"Honey," Martin interrupted, "that's not the point."

They sat down at the table. The room seemed nearly empty now with both Michael and John away at school. Joey was missing, too. He lay on the living-room couch, an afghan tossed over him, watching them through half-closed eyes.

"You see, sports writers in the Midwest and out on the West Coast will probably vote for guys in their area," Marty explained.

"But that doesn't make sense," Jean protested. "If John is the best—"

"Okay. We know that. But those writers have seen John on TV, or maybe in some game films. But seeing a film isn't the same thing as being in the middle of all the excitement at a game. And that's where they've watched local players doing their stuff—at a game."

"Well, I think that's unfair," Joyce said.

Anne brought in a steaming ribroast.

"There it is," Dad said. "I knew I smelled something good."

"You!" Anne said, pleased but unable to resist kidding her husband. "You'd eat anything that wasn't moving fast. Joey? It's on the table."

Slowly, Joey turned back the afghan and got to his feet. He'd eaten almost nothing for breakfast—for two days, in fact—and he was pale and listless. He walked with obvious hesitation in his step and bent forward slightly as if his stomach bothered him. Anne and Dad watched without making obvious their concern as he joined them.

Marty was still analyzing John's chances. "There are running backs in the country who scored as much as John did. Some may be faster, a lot of them are bigger and the sports writers who didn't get to see him play firsthand have to go by what they read in the papers. Statistics."

"Statistics are proof," Jean said.

"Uh-huh. Maybe. But Mark Twain said there are three kinds of lies: plain lies, damn lies, and statistics."

"Martin!" Anne said, frowning.

"I didn't say it, Mark Twain did."

"Statistics are good enough for me," Joyce said.

"Look at it this way. Oh, thanks." Marty helped himself to the roast and passed the platter on. "Sports writers say, 'Sure. A hundred yards . . . against *who?*' They don't believe big-time football is played in the East anymore."

"You don't give sports writers enough credit," Dad said.

Joyce was happy to hear support for her side of the argument. "Then you think John's got a chance?"

He smiled with faint irony. "No," he said, "not much of one."

"Help yourselves, please," Anne said, passing the baked potatoes around the table. Jean put one on her plate and passed the bowl to Joey. "Joey? It's hot! Will you take it?"

Joey got to his feet and said quietly, "I don't feel

like eating. Can I be excused?" He turned and left the room.

"You go ahead and eat," Anne told the others. She rose to follow Joey upstairs.

"Well, I think it's amazing the awards John's already got," Jean said.

Marty agreed. "I'm with you, Jean. I'm just saying that he should have a crack at the Heisman, too, but I don't think he will. My guess is he'll come in about fifth."

"*Fifth!*" Joyce said. "Don't let Joey hear you say something like that."

"Oh, if *Joey* had a vote . . ."

The discussion continued amidst laughter.

Upstairs, Joey lay on his bed with his clothes on. Anne stood in the doorway. "After all these years, don't try to tell me you don't like my cooking."

"I'm not hungry, Mom."

Sitting on the edge of the bed, Anne rested a hand on Joey's forehead. "Do you feel sick to your stomach?"

"A little. But really, it's nothing special."

"The doctor said the new medicine shouldn't make you throw up so much."

"I'll be okay," Joey told her. "I'm just not hungry." He twisted away from her touch and rolled onto his side.

Anne wasn't certain how to take his reactions. His appetite came and went, like anyone's. But Joey so seldom complained that she couldn't tell whether he was only tired or actually in pain. She knew that it often helped to steer Joey onto some neutral topic of conversation and get his mind off his physical problems. Then she thought of something else, better even than 'neutral topics.' "Did Jean tell you Johnny's driving home tomorrow?"

Joey swung around, his face suddenly coming to life. "No kidding?"

"He has a project he's doing for school, something for his Law Enforcement course, and there's a man he has to talk with."

"Do you think he'll be finished by three o'clock?"

"Three o'clock? If . . . oh, Joey. You've got your doctor's appointment at three. You won't—"

"I know. Will John be done by then?"

"Why?"

His nausea forgotten, Joey offered an eager smile. "Because I've got plans for him," he said.

He was no more specific with John the next afternoon. All he said was, "Go to the hospital with me, will you?"

John stood in the kitchen doorway, notebooks in his hand. "Hey, wait till I sit down. I just got in."

"Please, John. Say yes," Joey begged.

When John looked at her for an explanation, Anne shrugged.

"Okay," John said. "I don't know why I turned off the engine." He dropped his notebooks on the kitchen table and went back out to the driveway. Joey circled him excitedly.

"Not even a hint?" John asked as he backed the car out onto the street.

"You'll see."

Joey said nothing further but grinned all the way to the hospital. Nothing John said made him open up. When they got there, he seized John's hand and dragged him into the building. They hurried down the quiet corridors, John extending his stride to keep pace with Joey. As they rounded a corner, they nearly collided with a gray-haired nurse's aide.

"Hi, Mrs. Bartlett. This is my brother John."

"I'm sorry," John said. "I think we're in a hurry." He waved an apology over his shoulder as Joey dragged him on.

Suddenly Joey slid to a stop, looking perplexed. "Hey! He's not here yet."

"Who?"

"Mark. Remember? I told you about him."

"Only about nine thousand times," John said. "If—"

"But he's not here yet. Most of the time he beats me."

"Now I get it. That's why you dragged me along. To see your friend Mark, right?"

Joey's impish grin returned. "Mark's never met any football players."

In mock amazement, John said, "No! None at all? What a sheltered life."

"And he asked me if I could get your autograph. No kidding, John. When he finds out I brought you in person, he's gonna go right off his gourd!"

"Yeah? I've met people who didn't get excited."

"Just a minute." Joey ducked out of the alcove and trotted quickly down the hall to the nurses' station. A slender black nurse looked up at his approach, a pencil stuck in her hair. "Hey Judy," he said. "Is Mark in one of the examining rooms?"

She bit her lip before answering. "Uh . . . what?"

"Mark. He almost always gets here before I do."

She saw John observing their conversation. "Well, why don't you have a seat, Joey?" She rose and rested a hand on Joey's shoulder. Then she turned him gently and urged him back along the corridor. Slight and delicate herself, she wasn't much bigger than Joey. From a distance she might have been mistaken for one of the children who spent so much time in this particular wing of the hospital.

"You want to meet my brother?" Joey asked her. "John, come here. This is Judy, she's one of my nurses."

John met them halfway. "Hi, Judy."

She was strangely tense, looking from John to his brother and back again. All she said was, "Hello."

"Has this one been giving you trouble?" John asked.

"I wonder if . . ." She stopped and said to Joey, "Could you excuse us for a minute?"

Joey was puzzled by her mood. He hesitated, hoping for an explanation. When none was forthcoming, he said, "Sure." He walked away and sat down, watching them.

John and the nurse went a few steps down the corridor where they spoke in a quiet undertone that Joey couldn't hear, their heads together. He had the uncomfortable feeling they were discussing him. He couldn't imagine what the two of them might have to say to each other. They were strangers; they had never met before. His confusion deepened when he saw Judy turn and walk back to her station. John stood pensive for a moment before he approached his brother, his face solemn and his hands jammed deep in his pockets.

"What was *that* all about?" Joey asked.

"She wanted to talk to me about Mark." John sat down next to Joey.

"What about him?"

After only a moment's hesitation, John said simply, "Mark died last Wednesday."

Joey's face showed no change of expression. There was no surprise, no shock, and there were no tears. His face might have been carved in stone. Then he turned away from John and stared straight ahead, hunting for the right words. "John . . . All the . . . kids I used to . . . come here with . . . Now, there are all new kids here." It was almost as though he was talking to himself.

John reached over to put his arm around Joey's shoulders, and they sat together in silence.

24

". . . Ninety-nine, one-hundred. Time's up, Joey." Jean crossed to the couch where Joey lay in his pajamas, a thermometer held between pursed lips. She pulled it out, studied it, smiled at Joey and reached down to pat his hand. "Anything I can get for you?"

He shook his head.

"It's no trouble, really. I've got my room cleaned, and Mom's out hanging the clothes. She doesn't need me now." When Joey didn't respond, she walked out through the kitchen to the back yard.

It was a rare December day. If snow is not common

in Philadelphia, rain and cold weather are. When the sky had gone gray in early November, Philadelphians had braced themselves against the expected four months of damp chill. But the sun began to play tricks with the season, and a week of warm weather—too late even to be called Indian summer—had brought people out to wash their cars, to bag and mulch their roses, and to wonder at the sun in the sky. The thermometer had reached 66 degrees and Anne had decided to hang her laundry outside rather than use the basement dryer. She'd always enjoyed the fragrance of sun-dried clothes.

Humming to herself, unable to sing through the clothespin clenched in her teeth, she was hanging a flapping bedsheet when Jean came out of the house.

"His temperature's one-oh-two," Jean said.

Anne felt a quick spasm of pain, a stabbing sensation she dreaded—and expected—every day. She took the clothespin out of her mouth and pinned up the other corner of the sheet.

Trying to reassure her mother, Jean said, "I don't think he's in much pain. At least he doesn't act like it."

Anne nodded gratefully. She reached down to pick up the empty wicker basket.

"He's had one-oh-two lots of times," Jean said.

"I know. And every time I've felt my heart stop, thinking this could be the . . ." She didn't finish the thought. Instead she shook off her mood and smiled at Jean. "Give me a hand?"

Jean nodded.

Inside the house, the phone rang. Joey was still lying on the couch. He looked toward the kitchen; someone would pick it up. But no one did. At the third ring he raised his head to call irritably, "Somebody answer the phone!" But the phone continued to ring.

"Will somebody *please* answer the phone?" Joey shouted.

Still no one picked up the receiver. Whoever was on the other end of the line wasn't going to accept silence as an answer, however. Joey pulled himself to his feet and walked painfully toward the kitchen.

Outdoors, Anne and Jean had finished hanging up the laundry when they heard the frantic call.

"Mom!" It was Joey. "Mom . . . *Mom!*"

The women turned in panic when they heard Joey's scream from the house. They dropped the laundry basket and raced toward the door. Before they were able to reach it, a flying ball of energy burst from the house and ran straight into them.

Anne grabbed Joey's arm. "What are you doing—"

"Mom, we *won!* We won! *We won!*" He danced around her, nearly throwing her off balance as he dragged at the sleeve of her sweater. "We won, *we won!*"

"What are you talking about? And why are you—"

"Heisman!" he shouted. "We won, we won the *Heisman!*"

Jean shouted with delight. "You're kidding! We won the *Heisman?*"

Anne was dazed. "I . . . How do you . . . Who said so?"

"Eddie's on the phone, he said we won it!" Joey turned and dashed for the house.

"You get inside, Joey. You're not dressed for . . ." But he was already gone. Anne and Jean followed quickly. The receiver still dangled from its cord.

Joey beat her to it, snatching it up. "Here, talk to him. He'll tell you." He intended to hold the receiver to her ear, but in his excitement, Joey thumped her on the forehead with it.

"Oww!" Anne ducked, more startled than hurt, then seized the waving receiver to protect herself from Joey's enthusiasm. "All right, I'll talk to him, just give me a chance." Rubbing her forehead, she composed herself, turning half away from Joey, who whirled around her in his own version of a victory dance before dashing from the kitchen.

"Eddie?"

Eddie O'Neill was calling from the office of John Morris, Director of Athletic Information at Penn State. There, in the outer office, a half-dozen teammates were already whooping it up. John Morris himself was in New York, and his secretary did her best to control the noisy celebration while she watched O'Neill on the phone.

"Did you hear?" O'Neill asked. "We won it."

"How do you know?" Anne motioned Jean closer to the phone and asked, "Where's Johnny?"

"In New York," Eddie said. "The all-American team's videotaping a TV show or something."

"Have you talked to him?" Anne was shouting to offset the din she could hear at the other end of the line.

"Hey, guys! Hold it down!" Eddie shouted. "Have I what?"

"Have you talked to Johnny yet?"

"No. The Heisman people called the athletic office here. It's official. He won it two to one over the next guy."

Anne smiled broadly. She could think of nothing to say that would express the pride and gratitude she felt. Then she heard the sound of water running upstairs. "Jean. Go up and see what's the matter with Joey."

Jean dashed up the stairs two at a time. She glanced into Joey's bedroom but didn't see him. She stopped in front of the closed bathroom door. "Joey?"

Joey didn't answer. She knocked. "Joey? Are you in there?" She waited.

The door opened. Joey stood there undressed, a towel protecting his modesty, wrapped around his waist and held firm with one tightly clenched fist. "What do you want?"

"What are you doing?"

"I am going to take a bath, what do you think?"

Jean was thunderstruck. "You're going to . . . ? Without being told?"

He gave her a look of injured dignity and closed the door in her face.

In the kitchen, Anne was still in conversation with Eddie O'Neill. The shouting in the background was louder than ever. "Enough!" she said. "I've got to hang up, I want to give Dad the news."

John Cappelletti, Sr., was cold-riveting panels on an aluminum door custom-made for the garage entrance of the large hotel his construction crew was working on. He walked over to the foreman's shack to check on the detail plan for the job. On his way he passed a transistor radio blaring shrilly atop a stack of lumber. The radio had been playing all morning, though he'd paid little attention to it. It was a normal background noise, like the traffic beyond the board fence that surrounded the construction site.

John Denver was singing "Rocky Mountain High" when an announcer's voice interrupted: "Big news for Philadelphia. It just came through on our sports wire. John Cappelletti, from right here in Upper Darby, has been named the winner of the 1973 Heisman Trophy as the outstanding college football player in the country. And how about that, Penn State fans?"

Dad froze in his tracks. He looked at the radio; he looked at the door he'd been working on. Calmly then, he laid his rivet gun atop the building materials beside the radio. He walked toward the foreman's shack.

Steve Barton had just emerged from the shack in his shirtsleeves, hardhat in one hand. He watched Dad approach. "Something you need, John?"

"Steve, I'd like to take the rest of the day off."

Barton was surprised. "Is anything wrong?"

"No. My boy just won the Heisman." Tears of pride shone in his eyes. He pointed at the radio.

The gesture confused the foreman, and it took him a moment to understand what he'd just been told. When the news reached his understanding, he let out a whoop and pounded Dad on the back, yelling, "Everybody! Listen to this! Johnny just won the Heisman!"

Heads rose. Power saws stopped. Tools were dropped. Then everyone offered congratulations, shaking John's hand, thumping him on the back and yelling their happiness in so many voices he couldn't respond to any single one of them. So he merely nodded, a smile on his face. Somehow he managed to work his way out of the excited knot of friends—now busy congratulating one another on the happy news—to begin the happy trip home.

At Penn State, Michael was in class when a friend hissed outside the doorway. "Psssst! Hey, Mike! Come here."

Michael looked around anxiously, not at all certain what was happening. He pointed at the hallway and got a nod of permission to leave. A moment later his shout, *"All right!"* echoed through the classroom, startling everyone and drawing a wave of laughter.

Marty heard the news at work. He called Joyce at once.

Jean learned about the award after one of her friends heard it on the car radio during her lunch hour.

The winner himself was the only member of the Cappelletti family who didn't yet know about the award he had won. Members of the AP all-American team had gone to New York on December 3 in order to videotape the Bob Hope show the next day.

They had other obligations as well. John was rooming with Tony Dorsett, running back from Pitt, and they went with the rest of the team to Central Park where they spent much of the morning posing for pictures. A photographer took several shots of the group in different settings and arrangements. One of his photos would become a cover for *Family Weekly,* the Sunday supplement magazine. In spite of the unseasonable warmth, few passersby stopped to gape at the photo session, and those who did soon tired of watching several tons of athletic manpower being harried by a scrawny photographer any one of the young men could have thrown like a javelin. If anyone from the Downtown Athletic Club—sponsors of the Heisman award —was trying to reach John that morning, he didn't get through. John was nowhere near a phone.

After the picture session the team went directly to

the NBC studios and took seats in the audience section while the technical crew set lights and a production assistant explained the taping sequence.

John Morris kept out of everyone's way in the control room where he could see the activity on all sides. He was one of the first in the studio to learn that John had won the Heisman. He had seen Coach Joe Paterno walk into the studio. He could think of only one reason for Paterno to make the trip to New York, and when he rapped on the glass and got Paterno's attention, his raised eyebrows earned him a confirming nod.

For Morris the next ten minutes seemed interminable. Excited for John, he couldn't wait to share the news with him—but he had to. And it was finally the floor manager who walked out between the cameras toward the audience to make the announcement:

"Fellows? Want to listen up a second?" he said. When he had their full attention, he said, "John Cappelletti has won the Heisman Trophy."

An instant cheer went up from the assembled players.

Lynn Swann said, "Tell us something we didn't know!" Everyone was applauding.

Morris ducked quickly out of the control room and followed Coach Paterno into the audience to embrace John and congratulate him. Then, along with Bob Hope, they piled into Hope's limousine for the exciting ride to the Downtown Athletic Club, where the official announcement would be made. There they crowded into an elevator, and rose to the reception room where the scene was again pandemonium.

Flashbulbs exploded against a bank of brilliant lights behind TV and newsreel cameras already waiting to film John's arrival. A crowd of reporters and well-wishers had gathered around the elevator doors, threatening to trap the four men inside. Neither Paterno's pleas nor Bob Hope's jokes could move them away. It was officials from the D.A.C. who finally plowed a path through the crowd and led the way to a pair of microphones for more photographs and a question-and-answer session.

John was elated, and confused, and eager to phone his family and share the good news. He was delayed, however, because immediately following the question-and-answer session—and more hands to shake than John had ever encountered before—there was a press luncheon: more questions, more photographs, more dependence on Bob Hope's practiced and casual glibness to cut short the confusion and get him out of there. Then, back to the limousine and a harried ride to the studio to tape John's segment for the television show.

His skit was a small piece about athletes and endorsements. It seemed to go on forever, but finally there was a break in the taping session. He walked out of the hot lights, still somewhat dazed.

"Phone?" Morris asked him. John nodded, and Morris pointed him to a telephone in the quietest corner of the studio.

It was then that John Cappelletti called home to make the surprise announcement, to pass on the news that everyone else in his family had known about for quite a long time.

25

Joey had appointed himself doorman. He welcomed friends, relatives and neighbors who crowded into the house to join the celebration underway. A few phone calls from Anne had helped spread the word. Joey was decked out in an appropriate uniform. He wore his Penn State jersey, the number 22 standing out bold on his chest—his number, and John's—"CAPPELLETTI" across the back.

The doorbell was in mid-ring as Joey pulled the door open to shout, "Come on in! Did you hear the news?"

Lloyd and Paula Stockton, neighbors from down the

block, nodded. The noise made an answer impossible. They handed Joey a bottle of wine and a cake. Joey led them inside through the crowd. In volume and excitement, the living room matched the Penn State locker room after a big win, but here *Joey* was at home.

The dining-room table was covered with food. Guests circulated, talking happily. It was an impromptu party, noisier and better than any planned celebration could have been. Marty poured wine while Joyce and Jean served at the table.

"Here. The Stocktons brought this," Joey said to Joyce. Then he ducked away again; no one was tending the front door.

In front of the gray-stone fireplace, Anne and Dad blinked nervously at facing a TV camera and the glaring lights behind it.

"Did you really expect anything like this when John started playing high school ball?" the newswoman asked.

"No, of course not," Dad said. "But John's got a lot of God-given ability, and there couldn't be anyone who works harder or is more dedicated."

The reporter brushed a lock of hair back from her forehead. "You sound like you're proud of him."

"We're proud of all our children," Anne said.

"But especially John, today," the interviewer persisted. "Wouldn't you say that?"

Dad nodded. "I'd say that's pretty accurate. But then, it's an exciting day for the whole family."

"Thank you very much, Mr. and Mrs. John Cappelletti, Sr." The woman faced the camera. "This is Carol Winchester, in the Cappelletti home in Upper Darby." The TV lights dimmed out and the Cappellettis were free to join their friends, still a bit dazzled. Above the excited babble in the room, they heard the ringing of the telephone.

"Big day, right, John?" a neighbor shook his hand.

"I knew it," a woman said. "I told Harry only last night it was going to happen."

"Never a doubt, Anne."

Everyone seemed to be speaking at once.

"How did you hear about it?" Laura Stockton asked.

Anne stopped beside her to explain.

In the kitchen, Joey had picked up the phone. "Hello?"

"Hi, Hoss."

He recognized the voice at once. "Hey, John, wait a sec." He covered the mouthpiece and said to Joyce, refilling a wicker basket with slices of bread, "Tell Mom and Dad it's John on the phone."

Hunched over the phone in the NBC studio, John said, "Did you hear the news?"

Joey tried, not very successfully, to sound blasé about the whole thing. "I wasn't surprised. I told you you'd do it."

"You sure did."

"I said so months ago, and you did it."

"Okay, okay," John laughed. "Can I talk to Mom and Dad?"

"Boy, you're lucky you're not here," Joey told him. "It's wall-to-wall people in this place." He glanced up as his mother and father appeared in the doorway.

"In a minute," Anne said over her shoulder to someone calling. "There's a phone call."

"Here they are, John. Mom, take the phone. It's John." Joey held out the receiver.

Anne fended off her excited youngest son. "Don't clonk me with it again," she said. A stiff-arm against his chest kept Joey at a safe distance; she reached out carefully to seize the waving receiver. "Johnny? How are you?"

"Pretty exciting news, huh, Mom?"

"Congratulations, Johnny. We're having a party."

"I can hear that," he said. "Sorry I didn't call before. We were right in the middle of taping this TV show. Is Dad home yet?"

"Yes, he's here." She motioned her husband closer, and by tilting the receiver she was able to let him listen in, too, their heads together.

"Hi, son. We're awful proud of you," Dad said.

"Have you got your trophy yet?" Anne asked.

"No. They give it to me at a banquet, December thirteenth. You'll have to wear a tux, Dad."

"Me? I haven't had one of those things on since your mother and I got married."

"Where's it going to be?" Anne asked him. "No wait, wait a minute." She waved at Jean who was passing the kitchen door. "Jeannie, come here, come here."

John said, "Here in New York, Mom. They want you all here for the banquet."

"Oh, Johnny. I don't think I could get everybody there. We'd have to—"

"Sure you can," Dad interrupted. "Don't worry about it, we'll be there. Tell him."

Anne turned to her husband, the phone ignored and hanging from her hand. "That's such a short time!" she protested. "I'll have to see about someone to stay with Joey, and—"

"Mom!" John's voice interrupted. "What do you mean, 'stay with Joey'? He's included."

Anne looked down into Joey's eyes, big and bright. She said into the phone, "I don't know, Johnny. He hasn't been feeling well for the past few days."

Joey tugged at her sleeve. "Are you talking about me?"

"Wait a minute, Joey."

" 'Cause if you're talking about me, I feel fine."

"Sure you do," Anne said. "You and your hundred and two fever." She laid a hand on his forehead . . . but felt no fever. Surprised, she checked again, this time intently. Then she looked at Dad and shook her head. "Well, you had it an hour ago," she said.

John Sr. reached down to ruffle Joey's curly hair. He grinned. No bug, no fever could compete with the Cappelletti spirit on a day like this.

26

On the December weekend before the Heisman Trophy banquet, John finally came home. He was exhausted—both from the season just completed and from all the post-season excitement. What he needed more than anything was rest, and quiet, and a chance to study.

Friends and family were still sharing the pleasure of his many post-season honors. A few of them skipped work to drop by, and others phoned the family with their congratulations. But what many of these people didn't understand was that John was still in the midst of a school term. The football season had ended—except for the bowl games—but classes had not. John needed peace and a chance to study in surroundings quieter than the fraternity house would give him. There he was quarry for roving reporters, who hunted him down or phoned at all hours, badgering him endlessly.

His parents made certain that Jean and Joey gave him breathing space. After the first unavoidable few minutes of cheering celebration, they stayed away from him. Jean pledged to keep her high school friends away, but several popped in anyway, ostensibly to talk about school work with Jean but really to goggle at her handsome brother, vainly wandering through the house in search of a place to study.

Finally, he went into the den with his textbooks, made himself comfortable on the leather couch and stretched out, reclining on one elbow like a Roman emperor settling back for the orgy. But there were no dancing girls, no exotic feasts. A cored apple on a plate beside him, a reading lamp at one shoulder, his notebook open and his felt-tipped pen poised to write . . . he settled down to work.

He might as well have been back at the FIJI house.

Joey gave him a full thirty seconds of peace before barging into the den with a cardboard box that he put atop the television set. Then he darted out, returning with a pair of tablespoons that became drumsticks as he pounded out a thumping rhythm on the empty box, Joey's accompaniment, his own contribution, to the Penn State fight song.

John put up with the racket well into the fourth chorus, looking up in occasional veiled irritation, but finally he said, "Hey. Could the band play in another part of the house?"

Still Joey kept at it. He seemed to be operating on an enormously high energy level, literally unable to keep still. He dropped the spoons for a minute, picked them up again and went back to his thumping tattoo. Eventually, some vague feeling on the back of his neck made him turn around to find John observing him. Sheepishly, he laid down the spoons—quietly—and nodded quick agreement to John's unspoken request.

Then he stood with folded hands. His contrived silence was too pure to last long. "You want to go up and see the new car I got for my train?" he asked.

Engrossed in the book he was studying, John only shook his head.

"It's a tanker. It says 'New York Central' right on the side, and they've got the weight limits and everything."

John spoke calmly but firmly. "I just want to read this book, Joey."

"Why?"

"Because if I don't, I'm going to be in trouble Monday when I go in to take an exam."

It was a reasonable answer. Joey walked away—as far as the door, where he turned back to ask: "Do you like college?"

"Sure," John said. He answered without looking up. With his forefinger he traced a graph line, found the point he wanted, and jotted down a few notes.

"Better than high school?"

"Come on, Joey. Really."

Joey fidgeted for a moment. Then he picked up a

pair of magazines from the table at the other end of the couch, glanced at the covers and tossed them back toward the table. One of them missed and fell fluttering to the floor. Joey rubber-lipped a loud raspberry to imitate the sound it made falling. He skipped a couple of steps across the room and stopped to kick imaginary field goals. "Thirty yards!" he said, under his breath. "Forty!"

Place-kicking records broken, he turned on the television set. Instantly the sound of a siren filled the room, gunshots and a scream were heard and Joey hunkered down into a squat, staring at a police chase on the screen. That noise went on for a full minute.

"Joey!" John had to shout to be heard over the din. "I have to study!"

"Well, I want to watch TV."

"There's a TV set upstairs," John told him.

"Then why don't you study upstairs."

Blinking at the illogic of that answer, and trying his best to remain patient, John said, "Because I like this couch. And I like this light. And besides—I was here first."

"I like this TV better than the one upstairs."

John literally gritted his teeth and began to bundle up his study materials. He slipped his notebook inside the text to save his place, closed it, picked up the pen in one hand and rose.

Joey had been watching him out of the corner of his eye. When he saw that he was really driving John from the room, he quickly turned off the television. "Okay," he said. "If it matters so much to you."

Not certain it wasn't another game they were playing, John paused. But Joey sat contrite in the middle of the floor, his face innocent assurance, so John settled back on the couch. He opened his book again.

Joey wandered around the room. He picked two of the trophies off the shelf and clanged them together as if trying to break the heads off. Then he put them back.

A moment later he jerked the windowshade down to let it roll up and flutter, snapping like a machine gun.

Continuing his circuit, he picked up the fallen magazine from the floor, rolled it tightly and tossed it again toward the table. It opened in mid-air and settled slowly to the floor. The cover tore off. Joey flopped down beside it and folded the cover into a paper airplane, all the while humming to himself. When he had the airplane properly folded, he launched it. It made a big swooping circle against the ceiling, sailed down past John's face—missing him by no more than three inches —and smacked into the lampshade.

John hunched sideways on the couch, trying his best to ignore his brother. Silence reigned for one full minute—long enough to worry John, who turned around. Joey was watching him, waiting for his attention.

"Hey! Do you want to see the scrapbook Joyce has been keeping?"

"Later," John said.

Joey reached under the table at the other end of the couch to draw out the scrapbook; then he quickly flopped onto the couch. "It's mainly about you, John."

"That's nice." John continued to read.

"She's got everything in here about the whole season. Last year, too. All the newspaper articles and programs for the games, and ticket stubs. Why would anyone want to save ticket stubs?" When there was no answer, Joey said, "John?"

"I don't know."

"Don't you think that's dumb? Saving ticket stubs after you already used the tickets?"

John took a deep breath, trying to keep his patience. It wasn't getting any easier. "Yeah," he said. "That's dumb."

"That's what I told Joyce. Dumb. I'm going to tell her you said it was dumb, too."

"No, don't tell her that."

"Why not? If it was dumb, and you say it was dumb—"

John clapped his book shut. "Because I don't want to hurt her feelings, Joey. It was nice of her to do it."

"But you *do* think it's dumb. You just said so. And if you think it's—"

"Joey!" It was the end. John's patience, stretched beyond any imaginable limits, snapped. He slammed the book to the floor and yelled, "Joey, *I have to study!* Will you please turn your motor off and stop bugging me for just half an hour?"

Joey flinched as if he'd been slapped. He backed away, unable to meet John's eye, and bumped into his father in the doorway. Dad's presence seemed to heighten Joey's embarrassment. Without a word he slipped past his father and left the room.

John picked his book off the floor. He looked at his father and sighed. He wasn't proud of himself, but he hadn't been able to contain the frustration any longer.

"I can't blame you for losing your patience, John. But maybe you should know, he's on a different kind of medicine now. It makes him act . . . well, not like himself sometimes."

John nodded, his expression admitting that he'd already come to that conclusion, too late. All he could say was, "I'm thinking of trying out for a monster movie."

"Don't make a big thing out of it," his father said.

"Joey must know how I feel about him," John said. There was more than a note of questioning in his voice.

Dad entered the den to sit on the couch beside John. "Sure he does."

"But it's not always easy to say how you feel about somebody."

"I know," Dad said. "I sometimes wonder, myself. I know you kids love me, but I wonder sometimes what you think about the kind of father I've been." He turned to look at his son.

"Well, obviously we—"

Dad interrupted. "No, I don't want to talk about it now." His normally deep voice was suddenly light and throaty. "But I would like to talk about it sometime. You said it yourself, John. It's hard."

Nodding, John rose. "I'll go talk to Joey."

He was on his way upstairs when he caught sight of

Joey, sitting on the living-room couch. Joey was motionless, staring at the carpet at his feet.

John walked over to him without Joey's appearing to notice. "Sorry, Hoss," he said.

"It's okay." Joey was solemn, resignation in his voice.

"Things have been pretty hectic."

Joey nodded.

John waited for an answer that didn't come. "Let's go see your train," he suggested.

This time Joey shook his head.

"Please, Joey?"

"I don't want to."

"What do you say we run up to the Pike and get some ice cream?"

"No, thanks."

John sat on the couch beside him. "Hey, we're still friends, aren't we?"

"Sure." Joey's answer was simple and straightforward but lifeless. He might have been reciting a word in a foreign language, a word whose meaning he didn't know.

27

After the weekend, John had gone back to Penn State, prepared for the exam he had to take on Monday. Michael was already there. Their absence meant that Anne, readying the family for the two-day trip to New York, had only four people to pack for—Joey and Jean, her husband and herself. Dad often kidded her about the way she planned for dinner guests: if four people were expected, he said, she prepared enough food for eight . . . and then doubled it, just in case. Her packing followed the same rule of thumb. She was careful to choose the right clothes . . . and then an extra

outfit for each of them, in case someone spilled gravy
or tore something. In gathering all the necessary shirts,
shorts, socks and slacks, sorting them into the proper
suitcases, worrying about oversights she might have
made, she kept unusually busy right up to the last
day.

She was wearing a new dress and new shoes. She'd
had her hair done—with soft curling bangs over her
forehead and the back of her luxurious dark hair falling
free nearly to her shoulders. She was working under the
sort of urgent pressure she enjoyed. An ironing board
stood in the kitchen, clothes were folded and stacked
neatly on the kitchen table.

"John?" she called, as she walked upstairs. "Don't
you need special jewelry for your tux?"

He was in the bedroom, finishing his own packing.
"It came with the suit."

Anne walked in to join him. "Here's the shirt you
wanted." She straightened his half of the Samsonite
two-suiter lying open on their bed.

"Thanks."

"Don't forget the checkbook," she said.

"In my coat pocket."

She turned in a slow pirouette, making a last-minute
check. "Oh! What about your raincoat?"

"Anne, relax. It's only for two days, and . . ."
But he was speaking to her back.

She bustled down the hallway to Joey's room. About
to call him, she suddenly stopped cold. From her van-
tage point she could see Joey, though he hadn't yet
noticed her.

He was bent over a small suitcase, his slight weight
pressing down on it as he fumbled for the latch. His
hands to his stomach, he was doubled over in pain. He
stood there, bent over, breathing in quick shallow gasps.
His face gone dead white, he straightened up carefully
as if he were afraid of breaking something. His body
was taut. Then his breathing grew deeper as the cramp
passed. And at last, without a word, he took up his
labors again, his mother still unnoticed.

Stricken, Anne backed quietly into the hallway and

stopped two strides from Joey's door. It took an effort to gain her composure; the trembling hand she felt on her cheek might have belonged to someone else. She forced it to hang motionless at her side. When she spoke it was in a voice too loud and too bright to sound normal, but it was the best voice she could manage. "Joey? Did you remember your toothbrush?"

"In my suitcase," Joey said.

Fighting tears, she walked back to her bedroom and sat down on the bed.

Occupied, John Sr. didn't pay much attention to her. He latched the suitcase and tightened a drawstrap around it, pulled the belt tight and fastened the buckle. "What's wrong?" he asked.

"He's in bad pain today."

"Yeah, I know."

Now tears were sliding down her cheeks. He sat down beside her and pulled her head into the cradle of his shoulder.

"We were wrong," Anne said. "We were wrong to put him through so much."

He lifted her chin to be certain he had all her attention. "Anne, this is not the time."

"I mean it!" She jerked her head aside, refusing the comfort. "Can you tell me we did the right thing, when you see him like that?"

"Once you called it selfishness," her husband reminded her. "Maybe so. Maybe these last six years have been selfish of us, to want him with us. But think, Anne: if we've had him all this extra time, he's had us, too."

"But we didn't feel the pain! Was it right, what we did?"

Neither of them had a final answer. Slowly he took her in his arms and held her tight. Finally, the tension drained from her and she relaxed against him.

"Mom," Joey called. "I forgot to pack a sweater. Will I need one?"

The question brought her instantly out of her depression. The reassurance that Joey needed her was enough to bring the color back to her cheeks. It was

mere self-indulgence to feel worse than her son admitted
to feeling; that couldn't help him in any way.

Anne moved quickly to the closet out of sight of
the doorway in case Joey should enter unexpectedly.
"I guess not," she said. "As long as you have your jacket." She dried her eyes and brushed wrinkles out of
her skirt. Her calm was almost restored.

Dad kissed her lightly on the cheek. "We have to get
going."

She took a deep breath. "Do you have enough socks
in the bag?"

He smiled. "That's better," he said. "Take care of us,
will you?"

She nodded. "I'll be all right, John."

"I know." He took the suitcase off the bed, calling,
"Joey. Want me to carry your bag?"

Jean and Joey rode to New York in the family car
with their parents. Marty and Joyce planned to join
them later that evening, after Marty got off work.
Michael and John would be coming directly from
Penn State to the Downtown Athletic Club where
rooms awaited all of them. A reception and dinner
were planned for that evening. And the next night, in
the Grand Ballroom of the New York Hilton, the Heisman Trophy would be presented. The trip, exciting
enough for the ceremony alone, was also something of
a vacation, a chance to look around New York, to do
some shopping and to turn the unexpected early-winter
break in routine into a three-day holiday.

When they reached the Downtown Athletic Club,
after taking a few wrong turns on the southern tip of
Manhattan, their rooms were waiting for them. A bellman led them to their suite. He put their bags on a lug-
gage rack near the window.

"My, isn't this nice," Anne said.

Jean asked, "When are John and Mike going to get
here?"

"They said about one-thirty. They ought to be in the
hotel already."

The bellman opened the door to an adjoining room.

"Miss? I think this is your room in here." He looked at Dad, who nodded confirmation.

Jean dashed in to examine her room. "Joey," she shouted, "aren't you excited?"

Joey had walked to the window and was looking at the street nearly thirty stories below. "What are we going to do today?"

"The people from the Athletic Club are taking us shopping," Anne said.

"Where, Mom?" Jean asked.

"Wherever we want to go, I guess."

Dad walked to the door with the bellman and saw him out. There was a flurry of activity as they got themselves settled. Anne stripped off her coat. Jean carried her bag into the adjoining room. She examined the closets, opened bureau drawers and sang to herself as she toured the well-decorated room she would have to herself for the next two nights.

When Anne came out of the bathroom she was surprised to see Joey still wearing his heavy coat, standing at the window.

"Joey?" she asked. "Is anything wrong?"

"Do I have to go?"

"Go where?" His father hung his topcoat over a chair.

"I think he means shopping," Anne said. "What would you rather do, Joey?"

"I'll stay in the hotel."

With a look at her husband, Anne said, "Whatever you want."

"Hey Joey," said Jean, trying to spark some enthusiasm in him. "I'll bet the bellman doesn't know you're a celebrity."

"I'm not a celebrity. John's a celebrity." Joey didn't turn back to talk to her but pressed his forehead against the cool glass of the window. "I'm not anything at all."

He stood and watched the traffic far below.

28

"Where do *you* look when you're in one of these things?" Joyce asked.

"At the numbers, I guess," John said. He pointed at the light ticking its way left to right above the elevator door as they rose toward Joyce and Marty's room.

"I had a friend in school who used to drive people crazy. She'd get into an elevator and stand facing the rear of the car. They couldn't take it. They all stopped talking, and some of them even got out of the car, rather than ride with her."

John laughed. "For me, it was always in the dentist's chair. I never knew whether to look him in the eye, or go cross-eyed, trying to watch his hands." He pointed at the small parcels Joyce held in her arms. "Did you get everything you wanted?"

They had spent a few minutes talking with John's parents and Joey before going down to the lobby. In one of the gift shops there Joyce had picked up some lipstick and a few small gifts for friends back in Philadelphia. Both of them wanted to leave Marty alone to finish a task he'd taken on for John—organizing John's ideas for the acceptance speech he would have to make that night.

Joyce nodded. "If the people who run this place had known how many Cappellettis there are, they'd have given the Heisman to someone else."

"You mean, all the rooms they had to give us."

"That, and last night's buffet."

"I don't think you can call an Italian spread a 'buffet,' " John said. "Did you see all the food there?"

"Did I see it? I ate two of everything. And Michael sure did himself proud."

"I wonder what the word really is. 'Smorgasbord' is Norwegian, or Swedish, or something, isn't it?"

Joyce nodded. "And 'buffet' is French, I think. We'll ask Marty."

"Kind of tough on him," John said. "He comes up here to party with us for a couple of days, and I put him to work."

"No, he was glad to do it, John. It gave him a chance to show off a little. You know what writers are like."

"Anyway, I'm glad he thought of borrowing the typewriter from the desk downstairs." When the doors slid open, he motioned Joyce ahead of him.

As they entered the room, Marty was seated at the typewriter in his shirtsleeves, his fingers clicking a ragged tattoo, his tie hanging loose at his collar. "You timed that about right," he said, without looking up. "I'm nearly done. Want to take a look at what I've got so far?" He tapped a couple of pages lying on the desk.

John took them over to a chair by the window, and began to read.

"That means I keep quiet, I guess." Joyce hung her coat in the closet and watched the two brothers—Martin still typing, John reading the finished copy.

Finally, Marty stopped. His left hand lifted the page curled over the back of the typewriter to read what he'd written. He nodded, snatching the paper loose with a whirring sound. "There. See what you think," he said. He handed the last page to John and massaged the back of his neck and his shoulders.

"Marty, let me do that," Joyce said. She beckoned him closer. He sat on the bed beside her, twisting sideways, and she massaged his shoulders as John finished reading.

"Sounds good, Marty."

"It's up to you."

"I hadn't even thought about what I was going to say tonight," John admitted. "I'm lucky to have a brother who can write. Thanks."

"Not me," Marty said. "I just tried to put down what you told me. Say, you're not going to memorize that, are you?"

Rising from the chair, John walked over to the window. "Not a chance. I've heard too many dull lectures that somebody read to me. I'll sort of use it as a guide."

Marty patted Joyce's hand, a signal. "Thanks, honey," he said. "Feels good." He folded down his cuffs to button them. "Has it sunk in yet, John?"

Without turning around, John asked, "What?"

"Where you are. What's happened to you. You know what I mean."

John could only shrug. It had. And it hadn't. He knew what the newspapers said. And everyone he'd met had told him how he ought to be feeling--flattered, appreciative, thankful. Though all those feelings were present in his emotions, he felt as if he were watching someone else being feted by all the bigwigs he'd met in the past few days. It was very exciting, but it didn't seem quite real.

"I think the folks are still in shock," Marty said.

"Yeah. Me too, maybe."

"Mom seems to be enjoying it," Joyce said. "At least the shopping trip we took yesterday. You should have seen her eyes when we walked past that big display of candles in Macy's."

"That's Mom," Marty laughed. "Some women you'd expect to go crazy looking at fur coats. Show Mom some fancy candles or little cut-glass whatnots and her day's complete."

"Mine too," Joyce said. "Complete. I don't want anything now but a nap, if I'm going to keep my eyes open tonight."

Marty got up. "Think about it," he said. "Mom and Dad won't be able to move without bumping into ten celebrities. Imagine our family meeting the Vice President of the United States."

John looked out the window, preoccupied with his own thoughts. Thirty stories below, at the tip of Manhattan, he could see the Staten Island ferry leading its gentle wake. Off to the left, just a glimpse of Battery Park was visible. And behind him and to his right was all of New York City, with millions of people who had never heard of John Cappelletti, who even after the banquet that night wouldn't give him and his football records more than a passing thought over breakfast coffee as they noticed—or didn't notice—the small item about it in the newspaper. He was proud of his achievements, but the words of former Heisman winners were echoing in his head: to receive the Heisman marked an end to one career. Another lay ahead, as yet undefined, uncertain . . .

The past was important, but already accomplished. The banquet that night would mark a culmination. What would come next? What future could he plan for, or count on? Today he had his family with him to share in his pleasure, as they had shared in his achievement, in his earning the very right to stand where he was. Tomorrow . . . ?

John turned and strode to the desk. He sat down and picked up a pencil. Then, scribbling briefly, he wrote something quickly on the last page.

"Are you changing something in the speech?" Marty asked.

"Just adding a note," John said. He looked at the words he'd written: "Something special."

29

It was the first time that the presentation of the Heisman Trophy was taking place in the Grand Ballroom of the New York Hilton Hotel. This was the fortieth presentation, and over the years crowds at the annual banquet had grown and grown until facilities at the Downtown Athletic Club could no longer accommodate everyone who wanted to attend. On a long raised dais sat scores of celebrities, including former Heisman winners, football coaches, politicians, sports writers and broadcasters, officials of the D.A.C., guests, and speakers for the evening.

At floor level, two steps below the dais, the other guests sat at tables for eight or ten, those tables ranked

in rows stretching end to end under six brilliantly sparkling crystal chandeliers. With dinner already underway, there were nearly 4,000 people in the room,
most of the men in black tie, the women in cocktail
dresses or evening gowns. The tables were splendid, set
with crisp white tablecloths and linen napkins, polished silverware, sparkling cut-glass and brilliant floral
centerpieces.

The guests were relaxed and light-hearted, enjoying
dinner, calling out to friends who passed their tables
or sat within earshot. No tables were noisy, but when
4,000 people are quiet, their very murmurs collect and
build volume to a minor roar. Like distant surf—and
not too distant at that—the drone of conversation
ebbed and crested through the room, now and then
punctuated by tinkling glass and the bright cascade of
laughter. Liveried waiters passed among the tables.

The Cappelletti family shared a table directly below
the speaker's lectern, where they had a good view of
John seated just to the right of the microphone between two white-haired, suntanned gentlemen—execu-
tives of the Downtown Athletic Club. Vice President Gerald Ford sat on the other side of the lectern
from John—only a week after his confirmation as Vice
President. Long years of service in Congress had
accustomed him to affairs like this. He himself had
been a football player. The Cappellettis had been told
of his presence—he was the principal speaker for the
evening—and several unobtrusive Secret Service men
at the main entrance to the ballroom and standing
behind Vice President Ford on the dais itself made
clearer the man's celebrity.

But Vice President Ford wasn't the most famous
face. Michael had put it best, after an awe-struck moment or two. He leaned over to say to his father, "I
think I'm the only one here I don't recognize."

Joey was solemn—on his best adult behavior. There
were no other children in attendance, and very few
women. Coach Paterno's wife Sue shared a table with
John and Kitty Morris, in full view of her husband
seated at the long main table. Because the crowd was

so predominantly male, the Cappelletti table stood out: Anne in a black-skirted, white-topped evening gown, her eyes glistening brightly; Jean, with her dark hair tumbling richly to her shoulders and her cheeks glowing in excitement; and across the table next to Marty, Joyce, the only blond member of the Cappelletti family. With three such attractive women at one table, and with Michael, his father, and Martin there—all of them resembling John clearly enough, other diners in the ballroom had no difficulty at all in picking out the happy family.

Joey nudged his father to say, "There's Eddie O'Neill, Dad. See him?" Eddie returned Joey's wave.

Throughout the meal the family enjoyed identifying celebrities. They had met many of them during the preceding day and a half. Former Heisman winners were there, from Johnny Rogers, the '72 selection, back in time to Angelo Bertelli—the '43 winner for Notre Dame—and beyond. Leon Hart was there, and sports personalities and broadcasters including Tom Harman and Don Criqui.

Speeches followed the meal. The master of ceremonies introduced many celebrities at the long table with him, and a number of them took a brief turn at the microphone. Former trophy winners commented on what the Heisman award had meant in their lives, how that single recognition, being chosen the nation's best football player, had affected them through the years —in athletics, for those who'd gone on to a career in professional football; in the business world for others. The recognition conveyed by that trophy would always evoke warm memories. Some of the winners spoke directly to John, sharing their own special knowledge. For each, winning the trophy had marked a high point in his life.

And all the while, lights were flashing periodically as highlights of the speeches were videotaped for later television presentation. Newsreel cameras whirred, and photographers darted this way and that.

It might have been the Academy Awards . . . with one crucial difference. Tonight the name of the winner was known to everyone. John Cappelletti sat at the head table, nodding occasionally, smiling. Now and then he looked down at his family. Once Eddie O'Neill caught his attention and mouthed a silent comment John couldn't read on his lips, but he knew it was undoubtedly a joke. To John's right, a few seats away, sat Joe Paterno. Earlier that day, he had described John to reporters as "the best player I ever coached." With praise like that echoing in his mind, with the congratulations of friends like Eddie O'Neill, with the loving pride of his family fixing him steadily in the spotlight of their smiles, John didn't need the trophy to make his night complete.

Still, he was nervous. He had yet to make his speech. Those folded sheets of paper, clutched out of sight beneath the table edge for quick, surreptitious glances during the meal, had grown damp in the grasp of his perspiring hands.

And at last the moment came: it was time for the presentation of the trophy. John rose, stepped to the microphone and accepted the Heisman Trophy from the master of ceremonies and from Vice President Ford. The trophy was in the form of a bronze statue of a running back, football tucked under one arm and the other extended behind him to ward off a tackler as he made a hard cut.

The heft of the trophy surprised him. Over a foot high and nearly two feet long, it weighed twenty-five pounds, and shone with a handsome patina.

As photographers flashed their lights, John tried not to blink. He held one corner of the trophy while Vice President Ford held another. Suddenly then, and much too soon, he was alone at the microphone. The noise level dropped to an expectant hush.

John took the notes from his jacket pocket and laid them on the lectern. He began to speak. Among the first things he spoke of was his gratitude to his team-mates. John's generosity and loyalty were well enough known to everyone else on the Penn State team—many of them present—for them to anticipate that he would share with them the credit for the award. But to give them nearly all the credit, as he went on in honest humility to do, was almost to deny his own part in the Penn State undefeated season. That, too, his teammates had expected, and Eddie O'Neill resolved to rag him about it later.

John thanked the coaches, particularly Paterno and Bob Phillips, the backfield coach who had worked so patiently with him when he made the conversion from defensive back to running back. A touch of embarrassment played over Coach Paterno's features as John recounted a recruiting trip the coach had made to the Cappelletti home. Paterno had walked into the house on one of those days when Joey was ill and lying on the living-room couch. Instead of selling John on the virtues of the Penn State football program, or emphasizing the education he would get there, the coach, apparently dismissing recruiting from his mind, had spent the evening talking with Joey, cheering him up and then—as John said in his speech—"enjoying a good Italian meal."

John began to talk about his family. "My mother and father," he said, then stopped as he was interrupted by applause. "My mother always cries at these things, so I'm going to try not to. A lot of people may have noticed that my legs are not as straight as arrows. At one time I couldn't even walk without tripping, but she brought me through it so I learned to walk. And to run." More polite applause.

"My father is a quiet man," John said. "He asked me the other day how I felt about him as a father, and I couldn't say much to him then, but there is no person I have more respect for than this man."

John Cappelletti Sr. tried to restrain the pleased smile that spread across his face.

His comment brought perfunctory clapping from the crowd. The people gathered had wined and dined pleasantly and were now politely waiting through the last ritual in a fairly long evening. No one was bored, but for many of them, sophisticated veterans of similar banquets and acceptance speeches, it was difficult to imagine anything new or particularly pertinent to them that a twenty-one-year-old could say. Cigars were lighted, people sipped from wine glasses and coffee cups, glanced around the room; a few leaned over to talk to a neighbor quietly. They weren't rude; nevertheless their applause wasn't much louder than the buzz that rose and fell in the huge ballroom.

"My brothers Martin and Michael," John continued, "and my sister Jean . . . well, they've always been behind me, and I can't express what that's meant."

Marty leaned close to Joyce and whispered, "I know I didn't type any of that."

Joey was gazing intently at John. A few people on the dais leaned back and shifted their chairs to make themselves more comfortable. A man seated near the lectern picked the napkin off his lap and rolled it carefully to lay it on the table beside his coffee cup— a signal that, for him, the evening was nearly over.

John blinked. In the glare of the bright lights he was looking down at the table where his family sat. His eyes came to rest on Joey, for the last time during his speech. He had to look away, unable to face his brother.

"The youngest member of our family," he continued, "my brother Joseph, is ill." He hesitated; a break in his voice caught the crowd's attention. He fought back the emotion welling inside him. "He has leukemia."

Unbidden, tears began to roll down his cheeks, though he made no move to touch or even to acknowledge them.

His simple statement of fact stunned the crowd. Absolute silence settled over them. Cigars lay abandoned in ashtrays, wine glasses were lowered gently to the table, and all eyes were turned to the rostrum. A few people rose as if they felt the impulse to approach and support John where he stood. They couldn't believe what they'd heard—no one makes an announcement like that, they told themselves.

Joey showed no reaction at all.

John struggled to find exactly the right words. This part of what he wanted to say, *had* to say, was unprepared. It was that "something special." He knew how he felt, and here, in front of all these people, he would have to find a way to express those feelings. In a voice thick with emotion he said, "If I could dedicate this trophy to him, if it could give him one day of happiness, it would all be worthwhile." His voice was trembling, threatening to break at any instant.

Distressed, Anne Cappelletti murmured, "No! Johnny, don't." Dad took hold of her hand to quiet her. "It's John's night," she said. *"His* night. He deserves it."

Uncomprehending, Joey stared up at his brother.

Spectators cleared their throats nervously and sat with clenched fists, willing John the strength to go on.

"They say I've shown courage on the football field, but . . ." A sob shook him but he choked it back. For one long moment he stood frozen as if he couldn't breathe. He filled his lungs, a shudder passing through his stocky frame, and the deep breath steadied him. "But for me it's only on the field, and only in the fall." Now tears were pouring down his cheeks but his voice was under better control. "Joey lives with pain all the time," he said. "His courage is round the clock."

Coach Paterno had taken out his handkerchief and lifted his glasses to dry his eyes. Completely unembarrassed, strangers felt their eyes fill and leaned forward as though to reach out to John. Only Joey sat granite-still, his gaze unwaveringly fixed on his brother.

"I want him to have this trophy," John said. "It's more his than mine, because he's been such an inspiration to me."

Slowly, in wonder, Anne shook her head. Her own cheeks glistened with tears. Joyce had buried her head in Marty's chest. Still Joey didn't understand; his were the only dry eyes in the hall as he looked up at John. He seemed to be mesmerized.

Once again, John tried desperately to keep his voice under control, but this time he failed, finally and completely. He broke down and wept. "Thank you for putting up with me tonight," he said, nearly unintelligible through the sobs that wracked him. Somehow he managed to find his seat. He sat down quickly and put his face in his hands.

Unnoticed by one another, perhaps unaware of it themselves, spectators had slowly begun to rise during John's final words. As he finished and fled from the microphone, every man and woman present stood applauding enthusiastically. Coach Paterno moved quickly to John's side and pulled him erect to lock his arms around him. Eddie O'Neill applauded wildly, openly weeping, unashamed of the tears that coursed down his cheeks.

Raising his voice, Joey spoke at last. "Dad, I don't understand."

"John gave you the trophy, son."

"But . . . but that's not fair!" Joey said. "It's his. He earned it."

Dad rested his hands on Joey's shoulders. "He wants you to have it, Joey."

Slowly, the meaning of his brother's gesture sank in. Then Joey, too, began to weep, smiling also, as his father pulled him into a firm embrace.

Unable to trust himself not to break down, the master of ceremonies said only, "Ladies and gentlemen, will you please remain standing for the benediction?"

Gradually the enormous crowd grew silent as Bishop Fulton J. Sheen approached the microphone. Looking over the standing figures, half-hidden in darkness, he said: "Tonight you have heard a speech from the heart, rather than from the lips. You have heard that triumph is made from sorrow, that John was made in part by Joseph. I was supposed to pronounce the blessing at this point, but you do not need a blessing tonight. God has blessed you in the person of John Cappelletti. Good night."

There was a moment of silence . . . followed by total bedlam as photographers rushed into position around the Cappelletti table. And suddenly Joey found himself the focus of all the attention.

"How do you feel, Joey?" one newsman asked.

Joey was radiant, his tears drying now. "I feel great!"

Flashbulbs popped, reporters shouted questions, and a crush of people surrounded Joey. Anne and Dad stepped back out of the way and looked on with wonder as Joey stood in the center of that incredible celebration, fielding questions and laughing with joy.

Anne took her husband's hand. Her face glowed with pride and delight. Joey's happiness seemed so perfect. She looked at her husband and nodded. They had made the right decision.

For the gift that John had given Joey made everything have meaning. The past six years of uncertainty and pain seemed justified in that one instant: when the love John felt for Joey and expressed so openly and fully, when the feeling the entire family shared suddenly focussed in one bright and shining moment—and Joey stood in the center of that wondering crowd, partly dazed by the glare of flashbulbs and sudden attention but secure and warm in the love of his family.

Joey reveled in the moment, holding court, a true celebrity at last. He answered a question that only he had heard in the uproar. "Well, I already have one trophy that I won in Pee Wee League," he said. "So I think I'll put my new trophy right next to that one, and . . ." He had to stop. Beyond the circle of reporters clustered around him he spotted his brother trying to push his way through the crowd.

Their eyes met. John paused to grin at Joey. Joey smiled back, a smile so vivid and bright it seemed to light up the entire room. He broke through the reporters and started to run toward John. Only waist-high to the admiring adults standing in his way, pushing them aside, he ran. John reached out to catch Joey under the arms and hoist him high in the air.

And then both of them—tears flowing freely now, neither one feeling anything but pride in the other—became the center of a widening circle as onlookers backed away to give them room and watch John hold Joey close to him. The boy clenched his arms tightly around John's neck and hugged him for all he was worth, a drowning child who had found a rock to cling to.

For those two, in their embrace, the noise of the crowd disappeared. The people nearby might have been thousands of miles away. For that particular instant, they were the only two people in the world. The grasp they held each other in was fierce, and tender. They held that embrace. It would last them forever.

Joey died on April 8, 1976. John was at his side.

EPILOGUE—FALL, 1977

After another summer, the snowcone stand beside the Arco station just off WestChester Pike is closed. Jean and Michael, and occasionally Anne, kept it open again this year. It looked much the same as it did when John and Joey spent their hot July and August days there, though the business has expanded. To snowcones, Jean has added water-ice and soft pretzels. Children from the Highland Park Elementary School and adults playing tennis and basketball on the courts across the street now regard it as an institution.

Martin is no longer a journalist. For self-satisfaction as well as economic reasons, he became a carpenter. Independent, contracting out his services, he now works with his hands, like his father.

Joyce teaches reading at the St. Laurence Elementary School, employed by the Upper Darby School Board in a federal program to help children with reading difficulties.

John is a running back for the Los Angeles Rams. Late last spring he married Betty Anne Berry, a delicately freckled blonde he had dated for two years in high school. They live in California.

Michael is in California, too. A 1977 graduate of Penn State with a major in English, he currently works in a restaurant while establishing California residency. Intending to become a teacher, he plans to attend graduate school next year.

Jean is in her final year of nursing studies at Lankenau Hospital, a few miles from her home. Her aim after graduation: to work in pediatrics.

Anne and John Cappelletti Sr. still live at the same address. On the wall beside the staircase leading from their living room to the second floor hang a pair of portraits that tell a story:

Each year, former football great Tommy McDonald paints a portrait of the Heisman Trophy winner. His painting of John hangs at the foot of the stairs. After completing it, McDonald spoke with Coach Paterno about doing his portrait as well. Instead, he painted Joey, whose portrait now hangs beside his brother John's, a gift to the Cappelletti family from John's college coach and friend, Joe Paterno. The two pictures offer an interesting contrast: John, an adult, is strong and square-jawed; Joey, smiling shyly, is pink-cheeked and youthful. But the resemblance between the two portraits, hung side by side as they are, suggests the adult Joey might have become.

Anne and Dad show the justifiable pride they have in all their children. On the mantel above the stone fireplace in the living room are high school and college graduation pictures, and wedding pictures, of the children. And there, centered on the mantelpiece, stands John's—and Joey's—Heisman Trophy.